THE BEST IS YET TO COME

Facing the Fears of Today With
God's Hope for Tomorrow

SARA BROYHILL ANDERSON

Contents

CONTENTS

"But, as it is written, What no eye has seen, nor ear heard, nor the heart of man imagined, what God has prepared for those who love Him."

~1 Corinthians 2:9

Acknowledgments
and Dedication

Thank you to the editorial team who poured their love for Christ and faithfulness to God into the manuscript. The book is dedicated to the elect, all those who have or will shift the focus of their lives onto our God behind the plan. Thanks to Him for ensuring our stories all end with the best.

INTRODUCTION

"And God shall wipe away all tears from their
eyes; and there shall be no more death, neither
sorrow, nor crying, neither shall there be any more
pain: for the former things are passed away."

~Revelation 21:4, KJV

I am not your typical theologian. I am a wife, mother of five, lawyer, and apologist. So, you might ask, why I set out to write a book on the future fulfillment of God's promises? As a Christian who received her training in apologetics and the law, I have a particular interest in the *Parousia,* or the Second Coming of Christ; not for its mystery and intrigue, but for its value in advocating for and defending the faith. Rest assured, you do not need a background in apologetics to read and understand this book. The message herein is simple and universal. But for those who face hurdles to accepting the truth about God's plan, know that reason supports your effort.

If you are reading this book, you undoubtedly have some fear or curiosity about the future. I have a message from God, our Father, especially for you! Do not fear: *The Best Is Yet to Come!*

I was there once too. In the spring of 2002, as a young married couple, my husband and I took what was supposed to be a relaxing beach vacation to sunny Florida. While there, we stumbled across a TV special that examined the predictions of a man who notoriously foretold of events surrounding the impending "last days."

No surprise that the producers chose the end of the world as a topic for a television special. After the unpredictable terrorist attack on September 11, 2001, a new sense of insecurity settled into Western society. We wondered if these events could be a sign of God's coming judgment on the world.

I wasn't necessarily living altruistically at this point in my life. My sole focus was on my burgeoning legal career. Even though my desire was for the world, it hadn't always been that way. Jesus had made Himself known to me in unique ways throughout my childhood. In visions and dreams He had taught me to pray in His name, not to discount the schemes of the enemy, as well as to not focus on the past, but rather move forward in the direction of His promises.

However, for a moment in early adulthood my devotion grew cold due to failed attempts to please people and receive the validation from the professional world I felt I deserved. I wanted success more than I wanted salvation. In my naiveté, I decided to give God the silent treatment.

This may not come as a surprise to you, but when you box God out of your life, messages from the enemy about things such as death and destruction will fill the vacuum where God wants peace to reside. That night on our Florida vacation, fear welled in my heart as we sat glued to the images depicting a psychic's version of the end of the world.

As much as I wanted to relax, after watching the doomsday report about the apocalypse, I just couldn't. I slept little, replaying the dreadful "future." I decided to *try* to find peace on the beach the next morning. Little did I know I had packed the true message of hope in my suitcase.

A couple of weeks prior to our vacation I had randomly chosen a dozen books from a book club catalog. The books arrived the day before we left for our trip. When we were packing, I opened the box and haphazardly took the three on top for the trip. I didn't realize that one of them was about end time prophecy—only from the biblical perspective. Guess which one I unknowingly grabbed to read on the beach that morning?

Coincidence? I think not.

To my great relief, the *biblical* prophetic message was quite different from the ungodly one I had watched the previous evening. The book on biblical prophecy contained the best and most timely message of *hope*.

After reading it I realized that I had nothing to fear. I could relax. Since then, I have come to learn God's plan is the only one that matters. "For I know the plans I have for you, declares the Lord, plans for your welfare and not for evil, to give you a future and a hope" (Jer. 29:11). God has a wonderful, eternal plan for everyone who trusts in Him.

The direction of my life was forever changed. I fervently turned back to God and renewed my relationship with Him. Over the years, as my trust in God strengthened, so did my joy. Remarkably, my joy did not reflect the status of my circumstances; it *transcended* my circumstances. I had a newfound peace that could come only from God. No matter what happens on this earth, He is in control. If God is on our side, we have nothing to fear—not even the end of our time, or the end of all time.

> If God is on our side, we have nothing to fear—not even the end of our time, or the end of all time.

Interestingly, I had always believed that the name of the book I read on the beach in Florida was called *The Best Is Yet to Come.* I shared the book with a friend as soon as I came home, and in the years since I have tried to buy another copy. In fact, I had searched endlessly for it online to no avail. It was not until a happenstance encounter on the stacks of my local library that I reunited with the book I had read fifteen years prior. And even more interesting, although I recognized it right away, it was not entitled *The Best Is Yet to Come.* Written by Tim LaHaye, it was entitled *The Merciful God of Prophesy.*

All these years I had the wrong name for that book. In the same moment, I realized I had the *right* name for *this* book. God intended the title *The Best Is Yet to Come* for this project—a message for the end of the Age.

With all the events we have recently experienced that have turned our world—*your* world—upside down seemingly overnight, you might find yourself in the same place I was nearly twenty years ago. You are reading this because you too are worried about the future. You might also feel a spotlight shining on the state of your heart.

I pray that after reading the message that God gave me, you will no longer fear the events on the horizon. "And we know that all things work together for good to them that love God, to them who are the called according to his purpose" (Rom. 8:28). God wants us to know what's to come, and he will work it for our good. He wants to assure us that He has everything under control. We can trust Him to follow through on His word. We can have peace about God's judgment when we understand the God behind the judgment and the promise of the best future He wants us to experience.

> We can have peace about God's judgment when we understand the God behind the judgment and the promise of the best future He wants us to experience.

So who is this God behind the judgments at the end of the Age and on the judgment throne at the end of our lives? There are three components of God's character that can propel us into the future with joy no matter what unfolds (good or bad) in the world around us. Of all of God's traits, I will focus on these three in particular: *grace, justice,* and *hope.*

Because God does what He is and is what He does, He not only is grace, he gives grace. He not only is just, He enacts justice. He is hope; therefore, He secures hope. All of God's actions throughout history serve the purpose of carrying out the essence of God's holy grace, justice, and hope to carry us through the tribulations of this world and the trials of our lives.

Jesus said, "I have said these things to you, that in me you may have peace. In the world you will have tribulation. But take heart; I have overcome the world" (John 16:33). Suffice to say, the future has been written and it is a good one. Despite the turmoil in the world today and in our personal lives, we need not fear the future because our holy God guarantees that the best is yet to come for all those who put their faith in Him.

THE ELEPHANT IN THE ROOM

"For then there will be great tribulation, such as has not been from the beginning of the world until now, no, and never will be. And if those days had not been cut short, no human being would be saved. But for the sake of the elect those days will be cut short."

~Matthew 24:21–22

The "Best Is Yet to Come" may imply that there is nothing alarming prophesied in God's plan. Sadly, that is not the case. Before we move forward, let's address the elephant in the room—what may seem like I am trying to avoid with the adjective "best."

When I chose the title *The Best Is Yet To Come*, I did not do so because there is nothing dark on the horizon. I'm sure you've heard the phrase, 'It's always darkest before the dawn.' It means that things seem the worst right before they get better. So too,

God has planned a temporary judgment just in advance of the dawn of Christ's Second Coming.

We do not know when this period of judgment will occur. The Scripture opening this chapter describes it as occurring immediately preceding Christ's return to earth. However, we simply do not know when Jesus is returning. That said, Scripture foretells the scope of wrath to include events of unprecedented distress and destruction to judge those who have rejected God. The Old Testament prophet Daniel describes this period as "a time of trouble, such as never has been since there was a nation till that time" (Dan. 12:1). And in the Gospel of Matthew, Jesus says it will be a "great tribulation" (Matt. 24:21). Needless-to-say, this period will be marked by intense suffering.

Scripture discloses that no one would survive if those days were not shortened for the elect (Matt. 24:22). This is dreadful news to those who have not put their faith in Jesus Christ. So, why did I title a book about biblical end times the "best" is yet to come?

Because God's plan includes a "to be continued" for all those who choose to be on His winning team. Life for believers doesn't end with their mortal lives; it just *begins*. Jesus will return for His elect, those He knows will respond to His offer of grace. To contend that God's plan for humanity ends with *this* world undermines the holiness of God. When we focus on our temporary circumstances on earth, we miss the big picture of God's plan. We may only

> When we focus on our temporary circumstances on earth, we miss the big picture of God's plan.

know the here and now, but God has an eternal perspective on the future.

I, therefore, chose to focus on the best part of God's plan because this life is not the end of the story for those who accept God's offer to spend eternity with Him. If we choose God's path, we will have a place of peace to ride out the unpleasant seasons of life as well as a paradise of rest for eternity.

◈ TEMPORARY DARKNESS

There certainly are days that we feel this *has* to be the end. How could it get much worse? And I'm not even talking about the state of the world, I'm talking about the state of your own personal life. Your experience has left you gutted. How much longer can you endure? Illness, pain, suffering, losing loved ones, losing a job, humiliation, persecution, and the list goes on.

I've had unpleasant seasons in my life. I'm sure you have too. When the doctor told me a rare uterine disease had resurfaced in my body in the middle of my childbearing years, I was devastated. I already had three surgeries and two rounds of chemotherapy. We wanted to have more children too. The doctor, however, was adamant that he must remove my uterus immediately. His words knocked the wind out of me. My babies were the unconditional love in my life. In that instant, my universe turned dark.

The world has experienced some dark days too. When that happens on a large scale our personal suffering is compounded. The Black Death, French Revolution, Holocaust, and two World

Wars comprise a few examples in recent history when people likely hoped the day Jesus would return to save them was near.

But, this is now. And if you're like me, you feel another season of darkness eclipsing us. Once again, many people are focusing their eyes anew on the promise of the Lord coming back. Let's just look at some of the events of the infamous year 2020 when the reality we knew seemed to flip upside down overnight.

In late winter, the Covid-19 pandemic spread throughout the world, leading to lockdowns and quarantines. During this time, online news outlets reported increasing cases of physical and sexual abuse against children, human trafficking, anxiety, depression, suicide, and Covid-related deaths.

In late spring, the world lamented the death of a man who died during his arrest. The devastating act event awakened nationwide dialogue, understanding and outrage, protests and vigils, as well as riots and looting.

There are also growing numbers of despondent people searching for connection and meaning. Fear is rising in the hearts of people who are frightened of the novel virus that landed us here. Lockdowns and quarantines have changed the way we interact with friends and loved ones. Every time we think the pandemic has been contained, another surge keeps us from traveling for the sake of protecting those with health issues. Dark thoughts fueled by the fear of yet another lockdown or loss of freedom has the world living on the edge.

Then, there were the United States' elections.

The point is this: the world we know seems to be spiraling

down the drain of suffering and injustice, unknowns and distrust, relativity and immorality. When we look at what humans offer by way of answers to these problems, the solutions seem unreliable at best and unfeasible at worst. But if it seems like things are bad now, brace yourself, because they are about to get worse before they get better.

But, here's the good news: they *will* get better. The dark seasons of our life and even of the world—and definitely of God's judgments, are temporary for believers.

◈ TRIBULATION DARKNESS

I want to give you some context for understanding the judgments planned at the end of God's overarching design for the Church Age. This is an important part of understanding what is to come and why we are grateful that a perfectly loving God designed them—only His perfect love can cast out our fear.

In Daniel's timeline, the Great Tribulation period marks the end of the Church Age.[1] The Church Age denotes the centuries God has allotted for the Gentiles (non-Jews) to be grafted into the branch of faith (Rom. 11:11-31). Before the Church Age, faith was primarily reserved for God's chosen people, the Jews.

The Church Age began after Jesus's ascension into heaven and the arrival of the Holy Spirit at Pentecost. The Holy Spirit restrains the enemy during the Church Age, providing believers with the power to love, endure, and remain faithful to Jesus

---

1   See Daniel for a more thorough understanding of the Tribulation Period timeline.

even in the most harrowing circumstances. At the end of the Church Age, the Great Tribulation marks a span of time when humanity gets a glimpse of what existence on earth *might* be like *if* the restrainer of evil, the Holy Spirit, is absent.[2]

> The Holy Spirit restrains the enemy during the Church Age, providing believers with the power to love, endure, and remain faithful to Jesus even in the most harrowing circumstances.

According to the Book of Daniel, the entire Tribulation Period will last for one "week," or seven years. The Tribulation Period is the final "week" of seventy "weeks" prophesized to transpire before the end of the Church Age. Daniel 9:24-27 describes these seventy "sevens" or "weeks," which total 490 years.[3] This period began with the issuing of the decree "to restore and build Jerusalem" (9:25). Jerusalem was destroyed when Babylon conquered Judah around 586 BC. The decree to rebuild was issued by Cyrus king of Persia around the time of Nehemiah (2 Chr. 26:22). Scripture says seven "weeks" must pass before Jerusalem is done being rebuilt (9:25). It took exactly forty-nine years to rebuild the capital city. Scripture specifies that an additional sixty-two "weeks" are to pass before the Messiah is "cut off" (9:26). This was fulfilled at

---

2   Moody Bible Institute, "The Person and Work of the Holy Spirit," *moodybible.org*, accessed October 22, 2020, https://www.moodybible.org/beliefs/positional-statements/holy-spirit/.

3   "Seventy weeks are decreed about your people and your holy city, to finish the transgression, to put an end to sin, and to atone for iniquity, to bring in everlasting righteousness, to seal both vision and prophet, and to anoint a most holy place" (Daniel 9:24).

Jesus's crucifixion. That leaves the final "seven" of the seventy "sevens," which must come to pass before the end of the Church Age, and is understood to be the Tribulation Period.

When Israel rejected their Messiah, God set them aside for a season to graft in the Gentiles as beneficiaries to the covenants. Scholars interpret the Church Age as this special time for the Gentiles, and as such, do not count the Church Age against the progression of the 490 years. The final "seven," therefore, of the seventy "sevens" will begin at the time of God's sovereign choice.

We are alerted to the significance of the midpoint of this seven-year Tribulation Period by several events that mark its occurrence. First, a world leader will start the seven-year countdown by confirming a covenant with "many" at the beginning of the Tribulation Period "for one week" or seven years (Dan. 9:27).[4] At the midpoint of this seven-year period, "for half of the week," it seems he will break the covenant by putting "an end to sacrifice and offering," alerting believers to his true identity as the Antichrist, the "one who makes desolate" (Dan. 9:27). Jesus also highlights this event when he warns about seeing "the abomination of desolation spoken of by the prophet Daniel standing in the holy place (let the reader understand)" (Matt. 24:15).

"A time, times and half a time," is believed to represent a specific three and a half years, corresponding with the second

---

4   Could the covenant that is confirmed be the Abrahamic covenant, which provides the land grant to the nation of Israel?

half of the seven-year Tribulation Period.[5] The three and a half years is also represented by 1,290 days (Dan. 12:11). Sadly, it is this second half of the seven-year period, the Great Tribulation, that is associated with intense persecution unlike the earth has ever seen before.[6]

> "And I heard the man clothed in linen, who was above the waters of the stream; he raised his right hand and his left hand toward heaven and swore by him who lives that it would be for a time, times, and half a time, and that *when the shattering of the power of the holy people comes to an end* all these things would be finished" (Dan. 12:7, italics added).

The Book of Revelation describes three sets of "seven" plagues that angels unleash on the world during the Tribulation Period: Seals, Trumpets, and Bowls. The first four Seals are represented in apocalyptic imagery as four horsemen: the revelation of the Antichrist (rider on white horse), war (rider on

---

5   See Daniel 7:25, 12:7 and Revelation 12:14.

6   "For then there will be great tribulation, such as has not been from the beginning of the world until now, no, and never will be. And if those days had not been cut short, no human being would be saved. But for the sake of the elect those days will be cut short" (Matt. 24:21–22). "Here is a call for the endurance of the saints, those who keep the commandments of God and their faith in Jesus. And I heard a voice from heaven saying, 'Write this: Blessed are the dead who die in the Lord from now on'" (Rev. 14:12–13). "Then I saw thrones, and seated on them were those to whom the authority to judge was committed. Also I saw the souls of those who had been beheaded for the testimony of Jesus and for the word of God" (Rev. 20:4). "Then the dragon became furious with the woman and went off to make war on the rest of her offspring, on those who keep the commandments of God and hold to the testimony of Jesus" (Rev. 12:17).

red horse), famine (rider on black horse), and death (rider on pale horse). The fifth Seal shows the martyrs under the altar of God in heaven asking God how long they must wait before He avenges their death. They are told they must wait a little longer. The sixth Seal showcases catastrophic natural events taking place, such as a major earthquake, the sun being blackened, the moon turning blood red, and mountains and islands falling away. The result of these seal judgments: one-fourth of the world's population is eliminated.[7]

During the first three and a half years, the Antichrist manifests as a triumphant leader who brings peace and order to the world. He rules over a one-world government and economic system while his false prophet rules over a one-world religion.

The seventh Seal reveals something different: silence. Is God taking a rest as He did after creation? No one knows how long this pause will be. Perhaps it depends on the prayers of the saints. Perhaps a revival could emerge during this time. No details are given.

During the first three and a half years, the Antichrist manifests as a triumphant leader who brings peace and order to the world. He rules over a one-world government and economic system while his false prophet rules over a one-world religion. Daniel Chapters 2, 7, 9, and 12 as well as Revelation 13 and 17 give details on the empire of the Antichrist as well as the progression of empires throughout history that God used to further His purpose. The last empire before Jesus returns is made up of parts of a literal or figurative Roman Empire

---

7   See Revelation 6-8:1 for a description of the Seal judgments.

represented by iron, but mixed with clay, indicating both a strong and unstable power.[8] This empire is made up of ten nations who come together, yet give their power and authority to the Antichrist for a very short time.[9]

The next set of judgments is described as the "Trumpet" judgments. The first Trumpet includes hail and fire mixed with blood, resulting in one-third of the earth, one-third of the trees, and all of the green grass being burned up. The second Trumpet throws a burning mountain into the sea, turning one-third of all the ocean to blood, killing one-third of sea life, and destroying one-third of the ships. The third Trumpet reveals a star called wormwood, which causes one-third of the fresh water to be poisoned. The fourth Trumpet causes one-third of the moon, stars, and sun to be darkened. The fifth Trumpet unleashes terrible demon locusts with scorpion tails that sting and torment people for five months. Those who are stung wish for death but will not die. The sixth Trumpet judgment brings an angel to release the four fallen angels who kill one-third of mankind using fire, smoke, and sulfur from their mouths. Finally, the seventh Trumpet gives humanity another break in the judgments before the twenty-four elders declare that it is time to destroy those who destroy the earth.[10]

These judgments seem pretty dire, but the seven Bowl

---

8   See Daniel 2:36-45.

9   See Revelation 13 and 17:9-14.

10   See Revelation 8:6-13 and 9:1-21 and 11:15-19 for details about the Trumpet judgments.

judgments are even worse.[11] The first Bowl judgment inflicts harmful sores on those who take the Mark of the Beast to be able to buy or sell in the world marketplace. The second kills all remaining sea life. The third turns all the fresh water to blood. In the fourth, the sun scorches people with fire. The fifth covers the Antichrist's kingdom in a darkness so agonizing people gnaw their tongues in pain. The sixth Bowl dries up the river Euphrates to make way for the kings from the east. At this point, three unclean spirits assemble kings of the world for battle at Armageddon. At the seventh Bowl, there are heavenly signs of lighting, thunder, and the greatest earthquake that the world has ever experienced, splitting Jerusalem into three parts. Hailstones of about one hundred pounds each fall on people. Yet, people of the earth curse God rather than repent.

Please understand that the Bible speaks of an event that many people believe will be a "catching up" or "rapture" of the church in the air to meet Jesus Christ, potentially before He returns.[12] If this occurs before the Tribulation Period, or at least

---

11 See Revelation Chapter 16 for description of the Bowl judgments.

12 Some of the Scriptures that people point to about believers being removed from the Tribulation or Great Tribulation includes Revelation 3:10: "Because you have kept my word about patient endurance, I will keep you from the hour of trial that is coming on the whole world, to try those who dwell on the earth." Luke 17:34–37: "'I tell you, in that night there will be two in one bed. One will be taken and the other left. There will be two women grinding together. One will be taken and the other left.'" Revelation 7:14: "'These are the ones coming out of the great tribulation. They have washed their robes and made them white in the blood of the Lamb.'" 1 Thessalonians 4:16–17: "For the Lord himself will descend from heaven with a cry of command, with the voice of an archangel, and with the sound of the trumpet of God. And the dead in Christ will rise first.

before the Great Tribulation, believers will be spared the brunt of the Antichrist's tyranny. But even if believers are called to suffer or die for their faith, we do so knowing an even greater reward awaits us. "Jesus said, "Be faithful until death and I will give you the crown of life" (Rev. 2:10(c)). If believers are here for the Great Tribulation, whether they come to faith during this terrible time or the Rapture has not yet occurred, we need to set our eyes on God's promises and stay faithful to Him.

◈ ETERNAL DARKNESS

Compared to the time of unparalleled trouble, it is safe to say that, even despite the recent pandemic, the Western world presently lives in a time of unmatched prosperity, health, and freedom. Relatively speaking, it does not get much better than these modern times for convenience living. As bad as the 2008 housing bubble crash and Great Recession in the United States, most financial analysts agree the civilized world has a lot farther to fall before the slump gets close to the despair and suffering of the Great Depression. Yet even the Great Depression could be perceived by some as a moderate era compared to previous pandemics throughout the history of the world.

If we want to reach back in biblical history to find a terrible time of suffering, we need look no further than the exile of the Jews after the siege of the capital city of Israel (Samaria)

Then we who are alive, who are left, will be caught up together with them in the clouds to meet the Lord in the air, and so we will always be with the Lord."

by the Assyrians and the capital city of Judah (Jerusalem) by the Babylonians in the late seventh and sixth centuries B.C.[13] During the exile of Israel and Judah, starving people resorted to cannibalism to survive.[14] If we shudder to think of circumstances that compel such atrocities, we cannot imagine what the Antichrist has planned for the Great Tribulation.

Yet, Matthew Henry exhorts, "These are but the *beginning* of sorrows to those under the curse of God. What then will be the misery of that world where their worm dieth not, and their fire is not quenched!"[15] Please tell me that got your attention. Henry shudders to think of what *is* worse than even the worst time to ever occur in the history of the world. The answer? *An eternity apart from God.* "And if your eye causes you to sin, tear it out. It is better for you to enter the kingdom of God with one eye than with two eyes to be thrown into hell, 'where their worm does not die and the fire is not quenched'" (Mark 9:47–48). It's better to suffer here for a relative moment than suffer after this life for eternity.

In other words, if you associate death with the end of suffering, think again. "Surely it is beyond compare better to undergo all possible pain, hardship, and self-denial here, and to be happy for ever hereafter, than to enjoy all kinds of worldly

---

13   See 2 Kings 17:23-25 and 2 Kings 25:1-21.

14   2 Kings 6:28-30.

15   Matthew Henry, *Concise Commentary on the Whole Bible by Matthew Henry*, Biblehub.com, accessed May 28, 2016, http://biblehub.com/ commentaries/mhc/mark/9.htm (emphasis added).

pleasure for a season, and to be miserable for ever."[16] For those of you not certain about your salvation, suffering on earth is but the *beginning* of true pain.[17]

◈ LIGHT OF DAWN

We cannot escape the trials of this life, but we can choose to escape trials for *eternity*. His plan did not begin with a fallen world, nor will it end with a fallen world. The *end* is the culmination of reconciliation with our Father, our Creator, our Redeemer, and our Savior. That has been and always will be the best.

Don't take my word for it. Time and time again, the major and minor prophets of the Old Testament foretold of impending judgment. Both in near fulfillment and far fulfillment, these men, inspired by the Holy Spirit, prophesied distress as a result of disobedience. Their predictions, however, never stopped there. These prophets ended with a message of *hope* that (despite the judgment) the best is yet to come for those who trust in the Lord above all else.[18]

---

16   Matthew Henry, *Concise Commentary on the Whole Bible by Matthew Henry*, Biblehub.com, accessed May 28, 2016, http://biblehub.com/commentaries/mhc/mark/9.htm.

17   This is how you secure your salvation: "Because, if you confess with your mouth that Jesus is Lord and believe in your heart that God raised him from the dead, you will be saved" (Rom. 10:9). "And there is salvation in no one else, for there is no other name under heaven given among men by which we must be saved" (Acts 4:12).

18   For example, the book of Isaiah offers hope for God's people. God will judge Israel and Judah, but "Immanuel" was prophesied to establish a new

We struggle to understand how hope can exist in the midst of judgment. God, however, does not ask us to understand. He asks us to trust. Why? Because no matter how hard we try, no matter what our IQ is, no matter how much effort we exert, we simply cannot fathom our holy God. Scripture says, "How great is God—beyond our understanding!" (Job 36:26a, NIV). "His understanding no one can fathom" (Isa. 40:28b, NIV). We may not be able to comprehend all of the reasons God has planned what He has planned, but when we understand that His holiness requires that it all works for the good, we can have hope in the midst of this judgment.

So, will you trust God's plan or your own plan? I ask because even if you have a plan, do you have the power to execute that plan? And if so, are you sure you have the *best* plan?

Every day is one day closer to either the end of our life or the end of the Age. And while we await the day will come when Jesus returns to make all things right, as Christians have hoped for thousands of years, we also have to think about what Jesus's life, death, and resurrection means apart from that. Without even getting to the issue of the end of the world, Jesus's life has meaning for those of us who have to get through life's struggles of *today*.

> Every day is one day closer to either the end of our life or the end of the Age.

That's why it is important for us to focus on God's character. He is the one in control of world events. He is the one we can

---

Israel as God's kingdom on earth, righting the evil in the world. See Isaiah 1:19-20, 25-27; 7:14.

call on to get us through the events of our lives. Without an understanding of the author and perfector of our faith, fear will come. While we need not fear our circumstances, some fear *is* good—as long as it is the right kind of fear. Scripture teaches us that fear of God is the beginning of wisdom (Prov. 9:10). In the biblical view, this kind of fear is *beneficial*. Fear of God incites us to obedience and onto the narrow path to eternal life. Fear of God replaces fear of our circumstances with hope of eternity. Reverential fear of the Lord motivates a response from us—submission to His plan; because, whether we like His plan or not, we can trust it is the best plan.

As we begin to peel away the holy character of our incomparable, mighty God, fear of the future dissolves. In so doing we prepare our soul to trust the incomparable character of God in the midst of what could be perceived as "scary" circumstances. We begin to unpack what it means to have a holy God at the helm of end time prophecy and how His holiness makes all the difference in authoring a plan we can trust.

God has a plan for the future of humanity, but He also has set His eyes on you and your personal well being. "When you pass through the waters, I will be with you; and through the rivers, they shall not overwhelm you; when you walk through fire you shall not be burned, and the flame shall not consume you" (Isa. 43:2). I'd like to share one such experience that threatened to overwhelm me, but God used to confirm He was protecting me from the fire of my immediate trial.

My testimony started out as an exciting little construction project that turned into a nightmare. We fired our contractor, and he sued *us*. We now had to finagle how to pay for legal fees as well as the costs of the construction that had to be redone. To make matters worse, I had just been diagnosed with Gestational Trophoblastic Disease, a uterine disease that required chemotherapy and surgeries. I was exhausted, weak, and fearful. The stress was mounting. We were bouncing between hotels with three kids, balancing all of our responsibilities while trying to manage appointments with doctors as well as lawyers. Our faculties were stretched to the limit.

Before all this started we had planned a trip to Arizona as a Christmas gift for the family. On the eve of our trip, I couldn't sleep, so I slipped downstairs, making sure to barely turn on the overhead light so as to not wake anyone. With nothing else to do, I found myself instinctively reaching for my Bible. I had recently heard that a powerful way of worshipping is to read the Psalms out loud to God, inserting your name. It was a little awkward at first, but I did it and eventually I got lost in the moment. Suddenly, I felt an intense burning on my forehead. "That's strange," I thought. I looked at the overhead light set on low dimmers and wondered if the bulbs were intense enough to burn my forehead. When I realized they clearly were *not*, reverential fear flooded my body. Something out of the ordinary was happening. Suddenly, the fear I felt gave way to peace.

Later that day, as we were traveling to Arizona, I decided to pull out a Christian book my friend had gifted me called *Captive in Iran*.[19] What I read literally took my breath away.

---

19 Maryam Rostampour and Marziyeh Amirizadeh, *Captive in Iran: A Remarkable True Story of Hope and Triumph Amid the Horror of Tehran's*

The author, a new Christian, recounted the story about how she had experienced a burning on her forehead, as if God were branding her. I had never heard of such an encounter and now hers confirmed my own experience in the same day.

God had gotten my attention. He sees me, He has compassion on me, and He will be walking with me through this difficult time of persecution. I felt reassured that as I walk through the fire, I will not be burned and the flame of my ordeal will not consume me. I could rest in Him to find immediate peace that transcended my circumstance.

Friends, we may not all experience a burning on our forehead to tangibly remind us of God's presence in our suffering, but He is there none-the-less. "Fear not, for I am with you; be not dismayed, for I am your God; I will strengthen you, I will help you, I will uphold you with my righteous right hand" (Isa. 41:10). When the trials of life come, whether during the course of our lives or during the course of the Tribulation Period, we need not fear. God will not leave us or forsake us (1 Kings 8:57). We are not destined for wrath (1 Thess. 5:9). We may still be called to suffer for our faith, but we will not experience the wrath of those who reject Jesus and have to suffer eternal damnation. We have hope in God's promises.

Thus, when we study the end of the Age (or eschatology), we prepare our hearts for the inevitable conclusion of God's plan for our lives and for the world. We study prophecy on the premise that the supreme God of the universe does what He says and is the essence of what He does. We study Scripture so

Brutal Evin Prison (Carol Stream: Tyndale Momentum, 2013).

we can warn those not sealed by the Holy Spirit to prepare their hearts for Christ's imminent arrival. And we study God's promises to keep our eyes above the horizon of this world and onto the heavenly horizon to carry us through all of life's trials.

> God's plan *will* culminate with the doors to salvation closed once and for all. The question is: on which side of the door will you be?

There is urgency in understanding the imminence of Christ's return. God's plan *will* culminate with the doors to salvation closed once and for all. The question is: on which side of the door will you be?[20] Thus, while I do not discount the distress of the Last Days, I also do not want us to sell God's promises short. The holy character of God ensures He will fulfill His promises.

The bottom line: Jesus promises a "to be continued" when He states that "but for the sake of the elect, those days will be cut *short*" (Matt. 24:22, emphasis mine). And that continuation is better than we can even imagine. "What no eye has seen, nor ear heard, nor heart of man imagined, what God has prepared for those who love him" (1 Cor. 2:9). The best future is thus reserved for *you* to experience.

---

20 "I am the door. If anyone enters by me, he will be saved and will go in and out and find pasture" (John 10:9). "Behold, I stand at the door and knock. If anyone hears my voice and opens the door, I will come in to him and eat with him, and he with me" (Rev. 3:20).

HOUSTON, WE HAVE A PROBLEM

*"For as by a man came death, by a man has come
also the resurrection of the dead. For as in Adam
all die, so also in Christ shall all be made alive."*

~1 Corinthians 15:21–22

B efore we proceed with both God's judgment and the best that comes thereafter, let's establish the basis for it. How did we get here? We begin with a problem that God's plan of grace, justice, and hope solves.

The chapter's title "Houston, We Have a Problem" comes from a line made popular by the film *Apollo 13*. On that space flight, an unforeseen explosion crippled the spacecraft. The infamous statement conveys the real-life moment when the astronaut Jack Swigert made radio communication back to NASA Mission Control Center ("Houston") to inform them of the near catastrophic incident.

It turns out neither astronaut Swigert nor Mission Commander Lovell actually uttered these exact words. Nevertheless, due to popular culture, the phrase lives on and is used to informally mean *the emergence of an unforeseen problem*. And for that reason, it becomes a fitting phrase to describe the fall of humanity into sin.

At the beginning of creation, something caught the first man and woman by surprise. A problem lurked on the horizon; an "unforeseen explosion" loitered in the shadows of God's earthly abode. This problem sought to sabotage the people God created for the purpose of fulfilling their hearts' desire to worship Him and receive His eternal blessings. This enemy's ploy culminated in an incident that set the trajectory of human history.

God's plan begins in Genesis Chapter three, in the perfect garden God planted where He personally communed with the first man and the first woman.

> "And the Lord God planted a garden in Eden, in the east, and there he put the man whom he had formed. And out of the ground the Lord God made to spring up every tree that is pleasant to the sight and good for food" (Gen. 2:8–9a).

The Garden of Eden was truly a paradise on earth. The first man and woman enjoyed the perfect amount of light, water, food, warmth, and fellowship (not to mention, the presence of God in their midst). They had the freedom to enjoy the land as they were made with no shame of nakedness. God invoked only one limitation on their freedom:

"And the Lord God commanded the man saying,
'You may surely eat of every tree of the garden,
but of the tree of the knowledge of good and evil
you shall not eat, for in the day that you eat of it
you shall surely die'" (Gen. 2:16–17).

And that is when the unforeseen problem stepped out of the shadows.

"[The serpent] said to the woman, 'Did God
actually say, "You shall not eat of any tree in the
garden'?" (Gen. 3:1).

We might label Eve a little naïve. Up to this point, she had lived a sheltered existence. Nothing evil had penetrated her consciousness. She was not expecting a serpent with bad intentions to lead her astray. But then again, Eve already had the capacity to choose good or evil (because God created us with free will), even though she probably didn't anticipate being capable of actually following through. That is, until she was tempted. Eve answered the serpent with what God had told them, but she twisted God's words by adding an additional restriction, "neither shall you touch" the fruit (Gen 3:3). With the door opened, the serpent doubled down and twisted God's intentions.

"But the serpent said to the woman, 'You will
not surely die. For God knows that when you eat
of it your eyes will be opened, and you will be
like God, knowing good and evil'" (Gen. 3:4–5).

What happened next changed everything: a catastrophic clash of good and evil. Eve's free will—the exercise of her higher level of thinking and autonomy to make decisions—sampled the possibility of going her own way and relying on her own understanding. So she tasted the forbidden fruit and fell right into the trap of temptation.

> "So when the woman saw that the tree was good for food, and that it was a delight to the eyes, and that the tree was to be desired to make one wise, she took of its fruit and ate, and she also gave some to her husband who was with her, and he ate" (Gen. 3:6).

Adam and Eve suddenly had knowledge of good and evil. They noticed their nakedness and felt shame. Sin entered—and they had to exit. "He drove out the man, and at the east of the Garden of Eden he placed the cherubim and a flaming sword that turned every way to guard the way to the tree of life" (Gen. 3:24). Adam and Eve were ushered out of the Garden of Eden and into the barren world where they now had to toil for survival.

If the loss of God's physical provision was not bad enough, something much worse happened. The moment the forbidden fruit touched their lips, a great spiritual chasm opened between God and the beings He created in His image. This is the death that God said would result from their disobedience—spiritual death, the ultimate death that repeats for eternity.

"But the Lord God called to the man and said to him, 'Where are you?'" (Gen. 3:9). Why did God ask about their presence? God never loses sight of anyone. He definitely did not lose track of Adam and Eve. Adam and Eve hid from *God*.

We humans have a problem with divine coexistence due to our sin. God, too, has an issue with sin. God's holiness cannot mix with sin. "Your eyes are too pure to look on evil; you cannot tolerate wrongdoing" (Hab. 1:13(a)). Like the opposite sides of two magnets, holiness and sin can never touch.[21] Thus, the presence of God is more than physical; it is a spiritual presence that provides security and comfort as well as peace and significance in our hearts. Adam and Eve cowered away from God's presence as a result of their choice to disobey. God wanted them to know what they lost.

Sin works the same way today. Every human born after Adam and Eve inherited the sin Adam and Eve brought into the world through their disobedience. They broke the spiritual bond that once united them and us to God. Fear and shame now fill the vacuum where God intended His peace and love to reside.

Satan appealed to the couple's desire to be like their Creator to distract them from the blessings that flow from submitting to their Creator's care.

The serpent was Satan in disguise. Satan wanted Adam and Eve to focus on God's restrictions rather than on God's privileges. Satan wanted Adam and Eve to believe they were victims of God's oppression rather than benefactors of

---

21   See Exodus 3 for description of how God revealed Himself to Moses through the burning bush. Until Jesus and the Holy Spirit, God existed in the Tabernacle and Temple behind the curtain in the holy of holies.

His abounding generosity and love. Satan appealed to the couple's desire to be like their Creator to distract them from the blessings that flow from submitting to their Creator's care. Does this sound familiar in today's culture?

Adam and Eve were suffering from a case of entitlement. Entitlement can be the fruit of comparison and the dissatisfaction that comes therefrom. The dissatisfaction we feel from not having something valuable that we perceive others to have tempts the entitlement out of us. Ultimately entitlement stems from pride. Adam and Eve felt entitled to God's knowledge of good and evil. The serpent tempted their entitlement by stroking a level of dissatisfaction with the limitations God imposed on their existence. Guess what? The serpent is calling plays from the same playbook today—and it's still working.

What's the problem with entitlement, you ask? We hear a lot about "entitlements" from the government: social security, universal healthcare, and quality public education, to name a few. In addition, the bombardment of social media has elevated comparison to a whole new level. A profound sense of dissatisfaction has us trapped into feeling entitled to being satisfied. The question becomes, what can truly satisfy?

When we feel that we are "owed" something, being denied lights a fuse in us. We already have all that we need, but if someone has more (or just different), we believe we deserve it too. The attitude is so prevalent that Psychology Today has labeled the phenomenon the "Age of Entitlement." Its effects are substantial.

"When people feel entitled, they are not merely disappointed when others fail to accommodate their presumed rights, they feel cheated and wronged. They get angry, exude hostility, and assume a stronger sense of entitlement as compensation."[22]

A profound sense of dissatisfaction has us trapped into feeling entitled to being satisfied. The question becomes, what can truly satisfy?

Anyone who has been a child or parented a child (all of us) knows the anger that arouses in them when they are denied something they may have received in the past, or simply just want *now*. My friend posted a picture of her three-year-old son laying prostrate in the grocery store after she denied him a special treat. I've had my fair share of experiences with my own children. But perhaps my most vivid memory of entitlement was when I stole a Kit-Kat from the local grocery store at about the same age. The little devil on one shoulder won me over with the entitlement I felt for the chocolate indulgence, before the little angel on the other shoulder could convince me it was not mine to be enjoyed. It's cute when you're three, not so much when you're thirty-three or sixty-three.

How many times have you heard someone rationalize his or her entitlement with "I *deserve* to be happy." The story of a

22 Steven Stosny, "Anger in the Age of Entitlement: Entitlement and Anger Go Together," February 15, 2019, psychologytoday.com, accessed October 20, 2020, https://www.psychologytoday.com/us/blog/anger-in-the-age-entitlement/201902/anger-in-the-age-entitlement.

particular married couple speaks to this mindset. They told their marriage counselor that divorce was on the table. The wife just couldn't deny herself the happiness she deserved any longer. She justified her desire to separate from her husband by citing his lack of appreciation and constant demands. Turns out, her husband was just as upset. He worked all day at a job he didn't like and his wife never acknowledged his sacrifice. Patiently, the counselor listened to the couple's complaints about the other spouse until she interrupted. "You both have a bad case of entitlement. You feel entitled to actions *from* your spouse, but neither of you are acting *for* your spouse. Stop thinking about yourself and start thinking about each other."

It may surprise you, but even Christians are not entitled to a perfect life. God *gifts* believers a perfect eternity only through the merit of Jesus Christ, but we are not *entitled* to a perfect life. God simply doesn't offer entitlements. I am guilty of harboring a sense of entitlement that my children never get hurt or experience adversity. It's not pretty when we react to this entitlement.

No one is getting through this life unscathed. We are better off looking for a way to glorify God through the hurt. In fact, our testimony in adversity does more to further the kingdom of God than the pedestal we hoist ourselves on in times of blessing. C.S. Lewis says, "God whispers to us in our pleasures, speaks in our consciences, but shouts in our pains. It is his megaphone to rouse a deaf world."[23] Tempering our sense of

23 C.S. Lewis, *The Problem of Pain* (New York: Macmillan, 1962).

entitlement strips the enemy of his power by not letting him get a foothold in our lives.

An economics professor did a good job pointing out the effects of entitlements to his students. The professor conducted an experiment. For the next exam, he would average all the grades in the class. The ones who usually studied continued to do so. The ones who did not study, did not start. When the tests were averaged, everyone got a C. The high achievers were upset. The students who did not study were thrilled.

The students who studied felt entitled to a higher grade. The students who didn't study felt entitled to some of the high achievers' hard work. In the end, the high achievers grew less motivated to study while the other students continued not to study at all. None of the students had much incentive to work because they were not rewarded in proportion to their effort. The result—no one studied, and everyone eventually failed.

As the grades fell, the only thing that increased was the bickering and blaming amongst the students. Strife and division took hold. Sadly, that is where the road to entitlement leads: animosity and comparison, breeding more entitlement. The good news, there is an antidote: humility and gratitude.

When my daughter was five years old and in kindergarten, occasionally she would do something that would earn her a consequence. The day in question was one of those times. I decided she would have to forego treats as a result. At the playground that day after school, one of the moms talked about how she brought the class cupcakes to celebrate her daughter's birthday. I looked at my own daughter with accusing eyes. Of course, I was convinced she ate a cupcake. She was five.

Later, I asked her to choose an alternative consequence since she had eaten a cupcake for Emma's birthday. What she said next broke my heart. "Mom, I didn't have a cupcake. I knew Emma brought treats for her birthday so I saved a cheese stick from my lunch so I would have something to eat when everyone else ate the cupcakes."

I just cannot imagine what it took for my daughter to humbly accept her consequence and resist temptation to deny herself what she definitely wanted. She didn't feel entitled to the treat, so she let it go. She

> Spiritual death is far worse than physical death. Physical death separates us from loved ones. Spiritual death separates us from our Creator.

was grateful to have the cheese stick to distract her. No doubt there are other examples I could share of the opposite attitude, but in this example she taught me something of true humility.

My friends, humility is the antidote to entitlement: accepting what we cannot change and thanking God all the way through. Humility would have had Adam and Eve saying, "God is good. He only wants the best for us, even when He imposes limitations. I do not feel entitled to anything more than the good God has already gifted me." How much strife and sin would be avoided if we could muster a little humility and shed our sense of entitlement?

Sadly, when we rationalize our entitlement, we cast out humility, and we too pay a consequence. Paul tells us, "For as by a man came death . . . . For as in Adam all die" (1 Cor. 15:21–22). The moment Adam and Eve disobeyed God, sin opened the door to spiritual death.

Spiritual death is far worse than physical death. Physical death separates us from loved ones. Spiritual death separates us from our Creator. Sin is a major problem that we minimize and marginalize today. Sin and God's future plan cannot coexist. But God has a plan to deal with it. For those who submit to God, He promises a future where there is no death; where there is no sin. Redemption is assured for those who want to be free from their sin to experience the best that's yet to come.

CHAPTER

THREE

SPOILER ALERT

"I will put enmity between you and the woman, and
between your offspring and her offspring; he shall
bruise your head, and you shall bruise his heel."

~Genesis 3:15

Spoiler alert! God revealed the solution to the "unforeseen problem" immediately after it occurred.[24] Merely three chapters into the first book of the Bible and already our holy God discloses how it turns out. Like reading the last chapter of a mystery novel first, we know how the story ends: *God wins.*

If you were hoping for a suspenseful page-turner, will-it-happen-or-not, is-this-going-to-end-well storyline, you should ask for your money back. Future history has been set. The end has been written. And the climactic conclusion: the serpent will manage to merely crush the heel of Eve's Seed, while Eve's

---

24 Nothing is unforeseen to God. Only humans did not foresee that they could be tempted away from fellowship with their Creator.

Seed will fatally crush the serpent's head. The evil serpent takes a swing, but is ultimately no match for God's redemptive plan. God has purposed that Eve's descendants will have the privilege, power, and honor to finish the war that the serpent started when he tried to sabotage God's relationship with humanity.

Who is this Seed? And when will He crush the serpent's head? We continue into the biblical narrative to find out. In each ensuing chapter, we read about the lives of people and nations born from the line of Adam and Eve. Each generation accrues into hundreds of thousands of potential "seeds" that might materialize into the promised Savior. Likely, each generation hopes it will be the one to produce the Seed that will crush the serpent's head. With each birth, God's people cling to the expectation of the promise fulfilled.

In the generations after God banished Adam and Eve from His holy presence, the number of Eve's seed mushroomed. By the time one gets to the Book of Numbers, God's people had already grown to a force so formidable that God ordered Moses to take a census. The number of men aged twenty years or older eligible to fight in Israel's army: 603,550 (Num. 1:46).

As Moses tallied the troops, the thought that one of them could achieve God's objective to defeat Satan surely came to mind. If the enemy God intended to crush stood in front of them on the battle line, then all that they needed was a valiant fighter or clever military strategist. Yet none of the 603,550 troops measured up and completed the task of defeating the enemy. No matter how hard the troops tried, every single one of them fell short. The question became: Now what?

God's people put everything on the line in every battle trusting that the promise of victory over the serpent, their enemy, would finally be theirs. God's people diligently fought every war in an effort to fulfill the promise *their way*.

The battle, however, isn't *our way*. The battle will be fought and won *God's way*. His way is neither about physical domination nor about worldly status. The battle is not limited to a Middle Eastern field. The battle is not limited to specific peoples or nations. The battle is much bigger than our mortal minds can fathom. The battle between the serpent and the Seed boils down to an all-time, epic battle between a restored, eternal relationship with God or an eternity separated from God in hell—the place of weeping and gnashing of teeth. The Seed and the serpent are battling for where your soul will spend eternity.

Just today as I was putting the final touches on this chapter, I met a new friend who shared a testimony about just how real this spiritual battle is. My new friend, Rebecca, grew up in a Christian home with faithful parents. Her mom decided to follow Christ at a Billy Graham event. Her dad attended revivals early in life and was a believer. Thankfully, her father's faith came into play when he lived through a devastating stroke. He was able to call on the name of the Lord during a particular time of fear when he thought he might die. Doing so brought

> We have to shift our paradigm from focusing on our lives under the sun to our lives yet to come.

him peace from the assurance of knowing where he would go if this had turned out to be his end. Thankfully, God gave him another year on earth to spread the love of Christ with others before he went to be with the Lord for eternity.

To prepare for the end of our life or the end of the Age, we have to shift our paradigm from focusing on our lives under the sun to our lives yet to come. To ensure we receive the benefit of the *best* promised by the Seed's crushing of the serpent's head, we must acknowledge that we have a spiritual deficit caused by sin.

Spoiler alerts are bad if you like suspense, but good if you want to know you can trust God's plan. God provided spoiler alerts in order for both past and future generations to recognize the Seed and how His victory would play out. Isn't it amazing that everything happened exactly as foretold?

Around 700 B.C., the prophet Isaiah prophesied, "Therefore the Lord himself will give you a sign. Behold, the virgin shall conceive and bear a son, and shall call his name Immanuel" (Isa. 7:14).[25] A virgin conceiving a child might strike you as impossible. And it should. There is clearly a supernatural component to the mystery of how God would accomplish spiritual redemption through Eve's Seed. The Seed would possess a dual nature to both physically represent humanity to atone for their sin, but divinely do so once and for all time and for all people.

The prophet, Isaiah, foretold of the Seed's dual nature when

---

25 It was also prophesied that the Messiah would come from Bethlehem from the tribe of Judah. "But you, Bethlehem Ephrathah, though you are small among the clans of Judah, out of you will come for me one who will be ruler over Israel, whose origins are from of old, from ancient times" (Micah 5:2, NIV).

he called Him, *Immanuel,* which means "God with us" (Isa. 7:10; Matt. 1:23). God is with humanity in the closest sense. He came to *be* one of us by humbling himself to human form. Scripture confirms this historical fulfillment, "Great indeed, we confess, is the mystery of godliness: He was *manifested in the flesh . . ."* (1 Tim. 3:16). The Seed never lost His divinity in the process, but He did subordinate His divinity for the sake of accomplishing God's purpose to redeem us. The Seed's divinity gave Him the power to settle the supernatural score. His humanity gave Him the flesh to pay the price for our sin.[26]

Seven hundred years after Isaiah's Immanuel prophecy, a baby named Jesus was born in Bethlehem to a virgin named Mary.[27] This was no ordinary baby, but God's very own Son

---

26 "For indeed the enemy would not have been fairly vanquished, unless it had been a man born of a woman who conquered him. For it was by means of a woman that he got the advantage over man at first, setting himself up as man's opponent. And therefore does the Lord profess Himself to be the Son of man, comprising in Himself that original man out of whom the woman was fashioned, in order that, as our species went down to death through a vanquished man, so we may ascend to life again through a victorious one; and as through a man death received the palm of victory against us, so again by a man we may receive the palm against death" (St. Irenaeus, *Against Heresies*, Book V, 21, 1.)

27 "In the sixth month the angel Gabriel was sent from God to a city of Galilee named Nazareth, to a virgin betrothed to a man whose name was Joseph, of the house of David. And the virgin's name was Mary. And he came to her and said, 'Greetings, O favored one, the Lord is with you!' But she was greatly troubled at the saying, and tried to discern what sort of greeting this might be. And the angel said to her, 'Do not be afraid, Mary, for you have found favor with God. And behold, you will conceive in your womb and bear a son, and you shall call his name Jesus. He will be great and will be called the Son of the Most High. And the Lord God will give to him the throne of his father David, and he will reign over the house of Jacob forever, and of his Kingdom there will be no end'" (Luke 1:26–33).

sent to accomplish the mystery of the Promise. "But when the fullness of time had come, God sent forth His Son, born of a woman, born under the law" (Gal. 4:4). Jesus was the Seed who would do what no human to date could do—crush the head of the serpent.

Simply being born of a virgin, however, did not fulfill the whole Promise. The serpent must be able to bruise the Seed's heel. Isaiah also prophesied how this event would transpire hundreds of years before it actually happened.

> "He was despised and rejected by men, a man of sorrows and acquainted with grief; and as one from whom men hide their faces he was despised, and we esteemed him not. Surely he has borne our griefs and carried our sorrows; yet we esteemed him stricken, smitten by God, and afflicted. But he was pierced for our transgressions; he was crushed for our iniquities; upon him was the chastisement that brought us peace, and with his wounds we are healed" (Isa. 53:3–5).

Remarkably, as this prophecy foretold, the Seed would not come as a revered military leader. Neither would He arise as a sovereign dignitary clothed in royal garb. The people from whom he came would not recognize Him or receive Him. He would be rejected and despised; humiliated and crucified. If you were not familiar with Isaiah's prediction, the Seed might be easy to miss for lack of pomp and circumstance. Despite being divine, the Seed would lower Himself to death on our behalf, all while being rejected and despised by the very people He came to save.

Just as prophesied, the Seed died a gruesome and humiliating death: beaten, tortured, and crucified on a cross. They spit in His face, struck Him, whipped Him, pierced Him, and mocked Him until he gave up His last breath. "When Jesus had received the sour wine, he said, "It is finished," and he bowed his head and gave up his spirit" (John 19:30).

That is how the serpent was allowed to wound the Seed's heel. Thankfully, the plan does not end there. As prophesied: "Because you will not abandon me to the realm of the dead, nor will you let your faithful one see decay" (Ps. 16:10, NIV). The spiritual war was won when three days after His crucifixion on the cross, the Seed rose from the temporary place of the dead to sit at the right hand of God the Father in heaven. And spoiler alert, this was prophesied as well.

> "And [Jesus] said to them, 'Thus it is written, that the Christ should suffer and on the third day rise from the dead, and that repentance for the forgiveness of sins should be proclaimed in his name to all nations, beginning from Jerusalem'" (Luke 24:46–47).

It all went down just as predicted. "So then the Lord Jesus, after he had spoken to them, was taken up into heaven and sat down at the right hand of God" (Mark 16:19). On the third day after Jesus's burial, Mary Magdalene, as confirmed by the disciples Peter and John, found the stone that sealed Christ's tomb rolled away. And inside the tomb—*nothing but Jesus's burial cloths.*[28] As the angels standing guard at Jesus's tomb told the women, "He is not here, for he has risen, **as he said**" (Matt. 28:6a). "God raised him up, loosing the pangs of death, because it was not possible for him to be held by it" (Acts 2:24).

Perhaps these events are hard for you to believe. Consider this: Over five hundred people saw Jesus after He had walked out of the tomb and before He ascended into heaven.[29] And of the eleven disciples who witnessed Christ's resurrection, historical accounts claim that most if not all were willingly martyred rather than recant their testimonies.

So it was, in the fullness of time, after so many vain attempts by humans, that God effectuated *His* plan, *His* way. "But thanks be to God, who gives us the victory through our Lord Jesus Christ" (1 Cor. 15:57). Only Jesus, the Son of God and the Son of Man had the power to conquer the grave. No human can defeat spiritual death apart from Jesus Christ.

---

28   "Early on the first day of the week, while it was still dark, Mary Magdalene went to the tomb and saw that the stone had been removed from the entrance. So she came running to Simon Peter and the other disciple, the one Jesus loved. 'They have taken the Lord out of the tomb,' she said, 'and we do not know where they have put Him!' Then Peter and the other disciple set out for the tomb. The two were running together, but the other disciple outran Peter and reached the tomb first. He bent down and looked in at the linen cloths lying there, but he did not go in. Simon Peter arrived just after him. He entered the tomb and saw the linen cloths lying there. The cloth that had been around Jesus' head was rolled up, lying separate from the linen cloths. Then the other disciple, who had reached the tomb first, also went in. And he saw and believed. For they still did not understand from the Scripture that Jesus had to rise from the dead. Then the disciples returned to their homes" (John 20:1–10, BSB).

29   "Then he appeared to more than five hundred brothers at one time, most of whom are still alive, though some have fallen asleep" (1 Cor. 15:6).

Yet, that's not what we necessarily want to hear. Humans want a to-do list that we can check off line by line so we can maintain a level of control over the choice and timing of any religious obligations. It seems that every major religion other than Christianity provides this checklist. The problem: no two sets of guidelines are the same and none are straightforward.

The testimony of one young man who converted to Christianity drew my attention. He noted that the major factor that led to his conversion to Christianity was that Islam did not offer a clear path to salvation. "At one point it says all you have to do is believe. But then it also says you have to do so many other things so you can keep your status. And then, one day you still don't know where you're going."[30] This young man grew up in communist Albania where no one talked about God. When the iron curtain lifted, what was left was a post-Muslim nation with lukewarm adherents to any faith. Unlike so many of his peers, he wanted clarity about salvation. Thankfully, he continued to seek, and God was faithful to allow him to find the way, the truth, and the life. Discouragement over his constant shortfall was mitigated knowing the only One capable of perfection stood in his place to accomplish salvation on his behalf.

No matter how much we strive to measure up, humanity is left feeling inadequate. We inherently desire something more. We search, we innovate, we discover, and we solve; but regardless, the human mind is not capable of finding all the

---

30 Scott Rae, "From Islam to Christianity with Florenc Mene," *Think Biblically: Conversations on Faith and Culture*, January 24, 2019, accessed October 26, 2020, https://www.biola.edu/blogs/think-biblically/2019/from-islam-to-christianity.

answers apart from our Creator. There's only one clear path. That path eliminates checklists and innovation. The path is the same today as it was before time began. Why? Because people haven't changed, so the right plan hasn't either.

All humans are related to one man, Adam, through whom sin entered the human race. *All* humans also have the opportunity through one man, Jesus Christ, to receive the gift of redemption. The serpent tries to deceive us into believing that there are alternatives to God's way. But the serpent's agenda backfired. The serpent's attempt to kill Eve's Seed only succeeded in bruising the Seed's heel. In an about-face, the Seed's resurrection secured a glorious future for all those who accept the Seed's sacrifice on his or her behalf. God gave us the spoiler alert at the **beginning of time** (the Promise) to assure us that victory would come at the **fullness of time** (Christ's death and resurrection) to offer all of humanity the choice to accept full possession of God's glorious grace at the **end of time** (the New Jerusalem).

In the era since Christ's victory over death at the fullness of time, God has been patient to receive as many people who are willing to participate in His victory. God wants as many people as possible to choose His way to reconciliation. "The Lord is not slow to fulfill his promise as some count slowness, but is patient toward you, not wishing that any should perish, but that all should reach repentance" (2 Pet. 3:9). Jesus will not return until every nation has heard the Good News (that Jesus is the way, the truth, and the life), even if they do not choose to believe in Him as the way, the truth, and the life.[31]

In the interim, we partner with Christ as His people, ambassadors of heaven, to display His mercy and grace to the world. We labor on God's behalf, sharing the victory with as many people as possible so they can join the winning team before time runs out.

Rest assured, God's plan to completely eradicate the serpent will materialize and the perfect communion with God enjoyed for a time by Adam and Eve in the Garden of Eden will be restored. The time will come when Christ will crush the last enemy—death. When that happens, the door of opportunity to be saved will slam shut. The chasm between holy God and unholy humans—closed. Satan will be chained, loosed, and then thrown into the bottomless pit, never to return.

The serpent knows His days are numbered. And as his time on earth draws to a close, his efforts to divert God's children from their glorious reunion increase in proportion to his agitation. Thus, we must be ever more vigilant in our faith, keeping cognizant of God's promises for the future and armed for spiritual battle.[32]

---

31 "And this gospel of the kingdom will be proclaimed throughout the whole world as a testimony to all nations, and then the end will come" (Matt. 24:14).

32 See Ephesians 6:10–24 describing the armor of God.

CHAPTER
FOUR

Blessed Assurance

*"But, as it is written, What no eye has seen, nor
ear heard, nor the heart of man imagined, what
God has prepared for those who love Him."*

~1 Corinthians 2:9

W e cannot comprehend the glorious treasure
reserved for believers. What we see in this life,
in our world, is nothing compared to the future
God has planned. Even the best days and the prettiest views
pale in comparison to the peace and love that will saturate our
whole beings in heaven.

I recently picked up a book called *The Age of Extremes:
1919–1992.*[33] The author's examples underscore the radical
changes in the last century. For the minority who experienced
the extremes of power and prosperity, the pendulum swung
equally as high the other direction, where growing majorities
have experienced the extremes of poverty and oppression.

---

33   Eric Hobsbawm, *The Age of Extremes: 1914–1991* (London: Abacus, 1994).

As shocking as the author's observations, the scope of the book actually ended three decades ago. How much more extreme have the changes been since then?

The Covid-19 pandemic flipped our world on its head overnight. Now everyone is talking about the "new normal." But is this really what we want our normal to look like? Unemployment, isolation, loneliness, confusion, anger, oppression, and fear? If our world never returns to the "good 'ol days" before March 2020, will we find comfort? Yes. God has given us a blessed assurance through Jesus Christ, the Seed who crushes the serpent's head.

There's an old hymn entitled "Blessed Assurance." The lyrics start:

> "Blessed assurance, Jesus is mine;
> Oh, what a **foretaste of glory divine!**
> Heir of salvation, purchase of God,
> Born of the Spirit, washed in His blood."[34]

Have you heard the story behind the song? The iconic hymn was written by a woman named Franny Crosby. She wrote more hymns than anyone else during her 95 years on this earth—over 8,000. Anyone who could achieve so much must be extraordinary with no limitations, right? It may surprise you to learn that Franny lost her sight when she was only six weeks old due to medical error. She spent all of her life in darkness.

Yet she was no stranger to the light. Heavenly light emanated

---

34   Fanny Crosby, "Blessed Assurance," 1873.

from her Gospel hymns. She was quoted as having said, "I have a jewel – content." At age nine she wrote, "How many blessings I enjoy that other people don't. To weep and sigh because I'm blind, I cannot, and I won't."[35]

Franny believed in love even for "blind girls." In 1858, she married her husband, Van. Thereafter, the couple welcomed a child, but, as she said, "the angels came down and took our infant up to God."[36]

One day, her friend Mrs. Joseph Knapp asked Franny to listen to a tune she had written and tell her what the tune says. After kneeling in prayer, Franny announced, "It says, 'Blessed assurance, Jesus is mine!'"[37] She continued to dictate the hymn we know and love today:

> Chorus:
> "This is my story, this is my song,
> Praising my Savior, all the day long,
> This is my story, this is my song,
> Praising my Savior, all the day long."[38]

What Franny knew by "heart," we disbelieve on account of our "sight." Whether we choose to *see* it or not, we have been given a foretaste of the glory divine through the embodiment

35 Staugustine.com, "Story Behind the Song: 'Blessed Assurance,'" February 20, 2015, *The St. Augustine Record*, accessed October 22, 2020,https://www.google.com/amp/s/www.staugustine.com/article/20150220/LIFESTYLE/302209970%3ftemplate=ampart.

36 Ibid.

37 Ibid.

38 Fanny Crosby, "Blessed Assurance," 1873.

of God in Jesus Christ. In Jesus we see the glory of God and experience the fullness of His grace and truth.[39] Jesus is the visible manifestation of the invisible God. He came to be ours, to reunite us with Him. We access this blessed assurance because of God's grace through faith.

Like the Spirit, faith isn't visible to the naked eye. Jesus, however, converged the invisible with the visible. "Jesus said to him, "Have you believed because you have seen me? Blessed are those who have not seen and yet have believed'" (John 20:29).

And just as we trust what God has promised and secured through His visible Son, Jesus Christ, we believe Him when He promises incomprehensible peace, joy, perfection, and love for those who put their hope in him.

"Eye has not seen, nor ear heard, nor have entered into the heart of man the things which God has prepared for those who love Him" (1 Cor. 2:9, NKJV).

God has an amazing future planned, and we cannot even fathom how wonderful it will be. We trust it is everything God promises.

What about those in the world who do not have faith in the blessed assurance of something unseen? Their limited focus is on the here and now. Their eyes are focused on the present age of suffering and injustice. And their response to it lies in the power of their own limited understanding, leading to more suffering and injustice. What hope is there in that?

Jesus warned, "In the world you will have tribulation" (John 16:33). Jesus tells us to expect trouble. Death has not yet

---

39 See John 1:14.

been destroyed. Sin runs rampant and is rationalized away. We live in a fallen world. Living things decay, suffer, and die. The present world exists in rebellion to God and does not recognize Jesus as the way, the truth, and the life. "He was in the world, and the world was made through him, and the world did not know him" (John 1:10). Today, people are resistant to seeing in Jesus the good and loving God who came to sacrifice for them. Why?

> "Satan, who is the god of this world, has blinded the minds of those who don't believe. They are unable to see the glorious light of the Good news. They don't understand this message about the glory of Christ, who is the exact likeness of God" (2 Cor. 4:4, NLT).

The Holy Spirit can break through the darkness that clouds people's understanding of Jesus. Are you among those who incorrectly see Jesus? Perhaps to you He is nothing but a mere mortal? Or just a wise teacher? Do you blame Jesus for the world's failings? Or even the church's failings?

Jesus came so that everyone can see the glory of God and experience His grace and His truth. God's plan secured by Jesus Christ has secured a great future where there is no darkness. He has a plan for all those who are presently suffering and need to be healed and whole, loved and lifted up. "We serve a God who created our humanity, weeps at the fall of our humanity, became our humanity, and is redeeming our humanity."[40] Jesus

---

40 Glen Stanton of www.preachingtoday.com, quoted in Christianity Today International, *Crash Course on the Old Testament* (Cincinnati: Standard

came so that the wrong in the world will be set right in heaven. In His words, "Take heart; I have overcome the world" (John 16:33).

If this world were the end of the line, if this world were all God had to reveal about Himself and His love for us, then we would have reason to lose hope. Paul says it this way: "If the dead are not raised, 'Let us eat and drink, for tomorrow we die'" (1 Cor. 15:32b).

Thankfully, God's love story does not end with this world. The purpose of God's plan is to eliminate the source of suffering—ALL suffering—once and for all and reunite with His wayward creation for eternity. As Eugene Merrill states, "All history is an outworking of divine purpose, a purpose which, though apparently frustrated over and over by human disobedience, inexorably moves forward to a glorious and triumphant resolution."[41] God has planned the best to come for those who accept His gift of redemption.

> God's plan unfolds into an epic love story of sacrifice intended to restore our broken relationship with Him.

Thus, God's plan points to a future when evil that causes us to endure harrowing circumstances is *forever* eradicated. It points to a future that transcends the dreadful realities of the world as we know it. God's plan unfolds into an epic love

---

Publishing, 2008), 19.

41 Eugene Merrill, Mark F. Rooker, and Michael A. Grisanti, *The World and the Word: An Introduction to the Old Testament* (Nashville: B&H Academic, 2011), 275, accessed November 13, 2016, https://app.wordsearchbible. lifeway.com/workspace.

story of sacrifice intended to restore our broken relationship with Him. In God's all-out pursuit, He proves He is willing to move heaven and earth to accomplish reconciliation, our blessed assurance.

THE BEST TO COME

*"Come to me, all who labor and are heavy
laden, and I will give you rest."*

~Matthew 11:28

One thing life definitely does is exhaust. Just the worry of it all, even if we aren't presently experiencing any trouble, can spiral us down the drain of despair. The burden of this life is heavy. Jesus says we can give Him our heavy burden in exchange for an eternity of rest. Jesus Christ is the source of this peace of heart and mind. And it will fully manifest itself when all our worries are forever eradicated.

Here are seven things we can be assured are *not* present in heaven, making what God promises to be the best, truly *the best*.

◈ 1. NO MORE DEATH

So let's talk about spiritual death. What is spiritual death? When Adam and Eve disobeyed God, they opened the door to spiritual death. Spiritual death is far worse than the worst conditions on earth and far worse than physical death. Spiritual death isn't a once and done event. It doesn't last temporarily. You get no relief from it once you die physically. In fact, your misery only *begins* at your physical death and lasts for eternity.

Here's what Scripture has to say about spiritual death versus eternal life (bold added):

- "And these will go away into **eternal punishment**, but the righteous into eternal life" (Matt. 25:46).
- "They will suffer the punishment of **eternal destruction, away from the presence of the Lord** and from the glory of his might" (2 Thess. 1:9).
- "And if your hand causes you to sin, cut it off. It is better for you to enter life crippled than with two hands to go to **hell, to the unquenchable fire**" (Mark 9:43).
- "Just as Sodom and Gomorrah and the surrounding cities, which likewise indulged in sexual immorality and pursued unnatural desire, serve as an example by undergoing a **punishment of eternal fire**" (Jude 1:7).
- "Then he will say to those on his left, 'Depart from me, you cursed, into the **eternal fire prepared for the devil and his angels**'" (Matt. 25:41).

You might be tempted to rationalize away these dire warnings. You might not want to believe what God says happens after this life for those who do not accept His gift of grace through Jesus Christ. But for those who reject His path to eternal life, our wishes won't change the inevitable.

The good news for those who choose to take up their cross daily in response to God's grace is that God's plan destroys death. The scriptural warnings about spiritual death do not apply to you. His plan is as good as done because our holy God cannot go back on a promise. But He hasn't fully executed the plan yet. "The last enemy to be destroyed is death" (1 Cor. 15:26). The epic battle began when death became the consequence of man's sin. And the epic battle will end when God destroys death.

In place of spiritual death, Jesus offers a bridge to eternal life. That is forever (and ever) to spend in an unimaginable paradise with our Creator, who loves us so much He was willing to die so we can have this eternal life in heaven.

- "For the wages of sin is death, but the **free gift of God is eternal life** in Christ Jesus our Lord" (Rom. 6:23).
- "And **this is eternal life, that they know you, the only true God**, and Jesus Christ whom you have sent" (John 17:3).

Those with eternal life intimately know the one true God who sent Jesus Christ to atone for our sin. We know Him now through the presence of the Holy Spirit abiding in our hearts. But in heaven (the best to come), we will know Him face to face. Truly, intimately,

> The good news for those who choose to take up their cross daily in response to God's grace is that God's plan destroys death. The scriptural warnings about spiritual death do not apply to you.

knowing the immense saving love of our Creator, Savior, and Immanuel who humbled Himself to human form changes everything.

Can you imagine when you get to see Jesus face to face, letting His holy, pure, and sacrificial love wash over you as you embrace true love? True love never ends, never disappoints, never gives up, and never holds a grudge.

How does Jesus describe eternal life? "And he said to him, 'Truly, I say to you, today you will be with me in paradise.'" (Luke 23:43). What's your version of paradise? Do you equate this life to paradise?

You might have a great life of riches, fame, fortune, power, and popularity, but I bet you would admit that something is missing. The present shadows of paradise are but a mirage leading you down the path to nothing. The closer you seem to get, the further the satisfaction will veer from your grasp. But the paradise of eternal life satisfies all your desires because your true desire is communion with your Heavenly Father.

How do we get eternal life?

- "For God so loved the world, that He gave His only Son, that whoever **believes in Him** shall not perish but have **eternal life**" (John 3:16).
- "For 'everyone who **calls on the name of the Lord** will be saved'" (Rom. 10:13).
- "If we **confess our sins,** he is faithful and just to forgive us our sins and to cleanse us from all unrighteousness" (1 John 1:9).

Can we earn a spot in heaven? The Bible is clear—it is only by God's grace that we are saved. "For by grace you have been saved through faith. And this is not your own doing; it is the gift of God, not a result of works, so that no one may boast" (Eph. 2:8–9). Believers obey God and do good works. But works are the *fruit*, not the *root* of our salvation.

> Works are the *fruit*, not the *root* of our salvation.

No one deserves eternal life at the expense of God's very own Son. But because of God's grace, we receive it as a gift, not as compensation for our works. The righteous works by which we are judged are our acts of repentance with the imputation of Christ's righteousness. Without Christ to substitute for our works, we will be judged by the worst of our heart's motivations and actions.

That said, Christ also taught,

- "'Truly, truly, I say to you, whoever believes in me will also do the works that I do'" (John 14:12a).
- "'If you love me, you will keep my commandments'" (John 14:15).

Evidence of our salvation should abound in our good works, incited by a genuine desire to please God. Our good works don't get us an invitation to eternal life, but those who will be invited will do good works in response to what Jesus has done for them.

As the body of Christ on earth, we take on the responsibility of helping others experience the love of Christ through our works. If we have truly received the grace of God through faith, we want to do His will in response to the gift of grace He has given us.

◈ 2. NO MORE TEARS

What's better than knowing that Christ himself will right all the wrongs you have experienced in your life? "And after you have suffered a little while, the God of all grace, who has called you to his eternal glory in Christ, will himself restore, confirm, strengthen, and establish you" (1 Pet. 5:10). I have shed many tears: tears for others' suffering and tears for my own suffering. Because of what I have experienced in my life as a little girl, as a young woman, even as a mother of five children, I have much compassion for others who are sad.

I guarantee you have suffered. Some of your tears only God has seen. Your heart hurts knowing what you know, what you have seen, and what you have experienced. You cannot understand how a good God can allow such despair.

God doesn't want our suffering to last. Are you ready to stop crying? Are you tired of shedding tears over your troublesome past, the emptiness of your present, and the bleakness of your future? That's good, because God has a reprieve planned. Even in the midst of suffering, God gives us a deposit on the best that is to come to carry us through the sadness of this life in anticipation of the paradise to come. God himself will wipe the tears from your eyes.

If we perpetually look at our circumstances, however, we may never move past the memory or pattern of hurt. If we never look beyond the hurt, we will miss out on the joy promised to us right now. Did you know you don't have to have perfect circumstances for peace? Jesus offers peace that transcends our circumstances now as we look forward to the era of eternity where peace is the "new normal." "And the peace of God, which surpasses all understanding, will guard your hearts and your minds in Christ Jesus" (Phil. 4:7). Lasting peace is available through Jesus Christ.

As a historical figure, Jesus may seem remote or distant from you. Perhaps His death and resurrection seem irrelevant to your life right now. Let me assure you, nothing is more relevant to your present life and present sufferings than the Lord Jesus Christ. He knows you. He knows your sufferings. He wants you to take the path to reconciliation so you never have to experience those sufferings again. He wants you to be made whole and healed. The way is through Him to eternal life.

We may shed tears today, but they won't last if we look to the source of true peace. He'll give us a portion of His peace now as a down payment on what's to come—perfect and lasting peace, no tears. We don't have to muster it on our

We can look to Him now and allow Him to work through us to restore, confirm, strengthen, and establish us right now until we receive the full measure of peace in heaven.

own. God will give us His peace to change our perspective on our circumstances. We can look to Him now and allow Him to work through us to restore, confirm, strengthen, and establish us right now until we receive the full measure of peace in heaven.

◈ 3. NO MORE PAIN

Pain can be physical or emotional. Sometimes even emotional pain can be felt physically. I had a time of extreme emotional pain from the rejection of a loved one. During this time I felt a physical pain in my body. I believe this trial took its toll on my health. "For I consider that the sufferings of this present time are not worth comparing with the glory that is to be revealed to us" (Rom. 8:18).

It was in the midst of my emotional turmoil that I was diagnosed with a rare condition called a molar pregnancy, which metastasized into Gestational Trophoblastic Disease. After three surgeries, autoimmune side effects, and chemotherapy, I was physically healed, but it took me a while to be emotionally healed. God worked a miracle to change the heart of the loved one, but the pain left its marks both on my soul and on my body.

God was with me through it all.

He even communicated through the Holy Spirit to alert another believer to pray for me even though we had lost contact for over five years. When she called to say the Holy Spirit told her I was experiencing severe persecution, I broke down in tears. I prayed Isaiah 54:17 as she advised to push back on the spiritual warfare behind it all.[42]

---

42   Isaiah 54:17 says, "no weapon that is fashioned against you shall succeed, and you shall refute every tongue that rises against you in judgment. This

The point is that pain is real. We feel pain when someone hurts us. We feel pain when our bodies are injured. Some people, perhaps you, live with chronic pain. After a while no one comes around because there's nothing they can do for you.

Will it ever end? Is there light at the end of the tunnel? There is! His name is Jesus Christ. "He heals the brokenhearted and binds up their wounds" (Ps. 147:3). While you may not have total relief now, if you keep your eyes and faith on Jesus, you will have an eternity without any pain. You will have a body restored, glorified, with freedom you may never have experienced in this life.

> Is there light at the end of the tunnel? There is! His name is Jesus Christ.

I want to share a story from a friend of mine, Suzy, who has much experience leading and teaching Bible studies at her church. She wrote to me:

> "We all love stories of miraculous healing. However, we know that not all are healed—on earth. I have a beautiful story I would like to share: I knew a mom of 5 who was diagnosed with cancer. She had strong faith and told me, "God will heal me no matter what." Meaning, God would heal her cancer on earth or she

---

is the heritage of the servants of the LORD and their vindication from me, declares the LORD."
I prayed, "Heavenly Father, you are the great God who sees everything and everyone. You know our thoughts and our motivations. Protect me from the enemy. I claim your promise that no weapon formed against me shall prosper; that any word that rises in judgment against me You shall condemn. This is my heritage as a child of yours. My righteousness is from You. In Jesus's name, Amen."

would be healed in heaven. She went to be with the Lord, and yes indeed, she was healed. I think about the legacy she left her children; the peace of knowing their mother was at peace, healed."

The Bible teaches that no suffering in this life matters compared to the glory that will be revealed when we see Jesus face to face in paradise without any pain. Be encouraged to keep on keeping on in the face of your pain. "Therefore let those who suffer according to God's will entrust their souls to a faithful Creator while doing good" (1 Pet. 4:19). Endure present circumstances while still doing good. Pray for courage and strength each day to make it one day at a time until you receive your reward in heaven.

◈ 4. NO MORE TEMPTATION

This life is hard. We contend with temptation every choice we make. But it is not God who tempts us, but rather the enemy.

"Let no one say when he is tempted, 'I am being tempted by God,' for God cannot be tempted with evil, and he himself tempts no one. But each person is tempted when he is lured and enticed by his own desire. Then desire when it has conceived gives birth to sin, and sin when it is fully-grown brings forth death" (Jas. 1:13–15).

There is an enemy prowling around waiting to pounce if we give the slightest indication we are weak in an area. He offers thoughts we can either accept or reject, and the consequences of our choices are tangible.

Temptation feels good. Looks good. And the world tells us: therefore, it *is* good. But these are lies promulgated by the enemy who wants to divert worship from God. Our flesh is bent on evil ever since Eve and Adam gave into the serpent's temptation, and the result when we give in: spiritual death.

The Apostle Paul warns us, "But I am afraid that as the serpent deceived Eve by his cunning, your thoughts will be led astray from a sincere and pure devotion to Christ" (2 Cor. 11:3). God's plan is simple, but its simplicity in no way makes it ineffective. God's plan is exclusive, but that does not make it wrong. "Paul is warning us that Satan is going to use the same attack against us (and on our children, grandchildren, friends, family, and others) as he did against Eve to get us to a position of not believing."[43] Satan will try to convince us to doubt God's plan to save us from our sin and destroy death once and for all.

> While God has already won the war over death, the battle over sin continues to be fought in the hearts and minds of every person who rationalizes their sin.

While God has already won the war over death, the battle over sin continues to be fought in the hearts and minds of every person who rationalizes their sin. We are deceived into believing that we are all good people and that good people go to

43 Ken Ham, *The Lie: Evolution/Millions of Years* (Green Forest: Master Books, 2012), 23.

heaven. But the opposite is true. "The heart is deceitful above all things, and desperately sick; who can understand it?" (Jer. 17:9). Not one person is good enough to get into heaven and defeat spiritual death on his or her own merit.

The good news: God won the war! We only have to believe in Jesus and stay faithful in the face of adversity to have the Holy Spirit bring to mind the right choices that will lead us away from temptation and toward His grace.

In heaven, temptation will forever be eradicated because the source of temptation—our flesh, the world, and the devil—will not be present to corrupt our choices. Heaven is paradise for this reason. When we look around at the world full of people giving into temptation and thereby causing pain, tears, and suffering in the lives of others, we long for a perfect world where that option is eradicated. In the absence of temptation, we will be free to experience the best available to those who put their faith in Jesus Christ.

◆ 5. No More Hunger or Thirst

A discouraged woman sarcastically replied to one of my social media posts about God's unfailing love. She included a picture of emaciated children. "Except for these," she said, ". . . God hates these children." She posted a picture of starving children with the caption: "Thanks for your prayers; they were tasty and delicious." Her tongue-in-cheek remark was meant to highlight her perception of a hypocritical God who unfairly and capriciously doles out His blessings on some, while others are left to suffer.

How do we reconcile starving children with a good, all-powerful God? Shouldn't He save these children and others from their present condition and at least provide them with food and water to survive? "Jesus said to them, 'I am the bread of life; whoever comes to me shall not hunger, and whoever believes in me shall never thirst'" (John 6:35). Jesus said whoever believes in Him shall never hunger or thirst. Yet people, even believers and innocent children, starve to death.

Jesus was referring to Himself as the sustenance we need for spiritual life, or eternal life. Just like physical versus spiritual death, true survival is a spiritual matter. "Do not work for the food that perishes, but for the food that endures to eternal life, which the Son of Man will give to you. For on him God the Father has set his seal" (John 6:27). God doesn't want anyone to hunger or thirst. Yet the food and water that keeps us alive physically only points to the greater reality of what will keep us alive spiritually. That sustenance is Jesus, the bridge between our flesh and our faith. "I am the living bread that came down from heaven. If anyone eats of this bread, he will live forever. And the bread that I will give for the life of the world is my flesh" (John 6:51). "But whoever drinks of the water that I will give him will never be thirsty again. The water that I will give him will become in him a spring of water welling up to eternal life" (John 4:14). We worry about starving to death without food. Yet, feasting on the true bread and water of life will result in never thirsting or hungering again. Would you rather have temporary hunger and thirst or eternal hunger and thirst? Jesus is more concerned with your eternal needs.

◈ 6. NO MORE INJUSTICE

"So whatever you wish that others would do to you, do also to them, for this is the Law and the Prophets" (Matt. 7:12). A predominant worldview today categorizes relationships according to their power dynamic. Either you are with the powerful or you are with the powerless. Interestingly, Christians are sometimes seen to be part of the powerful because they have an allegiance to God above human government. They instead trust in their God as the power behind their lives (and eternities).

> Would you rather have temporary hunger and thirst or eternal hunger and thirst? Jesus is more concerned with your eternal needs.

Christians trust the God of justice. The truth is, humans don't have the requisite power, humility, selflessness, or knowledge to judge correctly. Often hindsight reveals even some well-meaning social justice movements backed the wrong side, becoming the oppressor rather than helping the oppressed.

We need not look too far back in popular culture for an example of misguided values. In the classic, *Huckleberry Finn* by Mark Twain, there is a scene where the boy, Huck, struggles with his conscience.[44] He turned a blind eye to allow his friend,

---

44   Mark Twain, *The Adventures Of Huckleberry Finn* (New York: Tom Doherty Associates, 1989).

Jim, to escape slavery. He wanted his friend to be free, but what was gnawing his conscience wasn't the fact that slavery existed. According to the social norms in his area at the time, he was bothered that he had betrayed his loyalty to Jim's "rightful owner."

The "right thing" for Huck to do has changed, and thankfully so. If he had gone with the cultural norms of his day, Huck might have made the wrong moral choice to contemporary audiences. Readers are relieved he did not.

We cannot always trust social norms telling us that a particular course of action is the "right" action. We have only to obey God, which is to love Him above all else and love our neighbor as ourselves.[45]

True justice requires a lot more than humans can bring to the justice table. We are called to seek justice. But true justice requires obedience to all of God's Word, not choosing to obey some and violate other laws. Justice calls for humility to treat others better than ourselves in every situation, never to victimize others in pursuit of our end goal. Those who do not treat others this way (even their enemies) and yet call themselves Christian do not represent Jesus.

How is God's justice different? God can serve justice because He always gives perfect notice, due process, and a fair hearing.

---

45   See Matthew 22:37–39.

a. Perfect Notice

Certainly there are many ridiculous laws on the books. Whether they are enforced is another question. We all know that ignorance of the law is no excuse, but the notion of being subjected to unknown standards violates our sense of justice. The point: notice matters. God gives perfect notice. "And now I have told you before it takes place, so that when it does take place you may believe" (John 14:29).

How does God give us notice of His law?

- "'I will put my law within them, and I will write it on their hearts. And I will be their God, and they shall be my people'" (Jer. 31:33).
- "For when the Gentiles, who do not have the law, by nature do what the law requires, they are a law to themselves, even though they do not have the law. They show that the work of the law is written on their hearts, while their conscience also bears witness, and their conflicting thoughts accuse or even excuse them" (Rom. 2:14–15).
- "For his invisible attributes, namely, his eternal power and divine nature, have been clearly perceived, ever since the creation of the world, in the things that have been made. So they are without excuse" (Rom. 1:20).

And as the Scripture from John 14:29 says, God himself tells us in advance through the prophets so when it comes true, we can believe He planned it. If the thought of memorizing all of

God's "laws" overwhelms you, take heart, the book is written on your heart. The Holy Spirit will bring them to mind so you know when to obey and when you are not obeying.

b. Speedy Due Process

Ever heard the phrase "justice delayed is justice denied"? Truly, justice cannot be adequately served without swift execution of due process. So what is God's version of "expedient" justice? "And will not God give justice to his elect, who cry out to him day and night? Will he delay long over them?" (Luke 18:7). While God's expedient justice may not be immediate justice, the Scripture above rhetorically makes the point that it will never result in justice denied. "I tell you, he will give justice to them speedily. Nevertheless, when the Son of Man comes, will he find faith on earth?" (Luke 18:8). The point is that "speedy due process" doesn't work if there's no one to save. Due process needs to be delayed enough to give people a chance to come to faith. God's justice delayed (by human standards) may be our only shot to prepare our hearts to receive His gift of grace through faith.

God patiently executes justice so that "the number of their fellow servants and their brothers should be complete" (Rev. 6:11). Justice delayed does not mean justice denied; it means holy justice *perfected.*

c. Fair Hearing

Lawsuits and legal charges are extremely stressful and rightfully so when we consider that other fallible humans hold our justice in their hands. God frowns upon lawsuits for this reason. Humans are fickle, self-interested, and easily distracted. Humans lie. How can we be assured of a fair hearing by an impartial judge and competent counsel? We have the most competent counsel to argue our case before God and ensure a fair trial.

Jesus, the Son of God, serves as our righteous counsel. "My little children, I am writing these things to you so that you may not sin. But if anyone does sin, we have an advocate with the Father, Jesus Christ the righteous" (1 John 2:1). As God, Jesus has all the benefits of holy omnibenevolence (all good), omniscience (all knowing), omnipresence (all places), and omnipotence (all powerful). And as the perfect advocate, He accepts His own unbreakable terms of justice. That's the best hearing of our case we could hope for.

> And as the perfect advocate, He accepts His own unbreakable terms of justice.

◈ 7. NO MORE LIES

Who knew one of the most dangerous threats facing our society today would be "fake news"? As we sit at home glued to the television and Internet to pass the time of social distancing and quarantine, we gasp at the vision of our fallen world on full display in panoramic proportion. Every person armed with an iPhone has become a reporter. Technology has enabled society to know the ins and outs of almost any corner of the universe at a moment's notice. Despite the wide array of views, however, we don't always get the full picture of any particular event.

What do those numerous lenses showcase? Extreme violence. Extreme hatred. Extreme debt. Extreme weather. Extreme fires. Extreme poverty. Extreme wealth. Extreme threats. Extreme persecution. Extreme intolerance. Extreme rhetoric. Extreme injustice.

It seems like we are a world balancing on the point of a needle. One talking head might have you believe the bubble that is the world economy could burst at any moment; another that the fickle finger of a rogue regime could trigger nuclear annihilation on a whim.

You would not be alone if the threat of any of the above leaves you scared to close your eyes at night. If you are like me, you want assurance that everything is going to be okay. Where do you go to find it? Technology? Or political rhetoric? Or government programs? Or conspiracy theorists?

We are bombarded with information every day. We can succumb to fear and anxiety, or we can methodically measure each sound bite against truth. Truth can be defined as the correspondence of a purported fact to reality. Reality is what is real. Real is what is true. Therefore truth and reality are not mutually exclusive; they go hand in hand.

Nothing gets me more worked up then hearing someone

say "that's my truth." Because what they're doing is justifying their opinion or belief that has no bearing on reality—and they know it. As if just owning a misconception makes it true. If everyone defines his or her own truth, then nothing is true because there's no objective basis against which to measure every truth. Even the statement that "nothing is true" doesn't hold up to this truth standard.

It may surprise you, but belief does not require truth. To be true, a statement or purported fact must correspond with reality. Much of the truth that Christianity points to relates to the unseen world, but that does not make it less real. The very question of "truth" is unseen, giving evidence of the unseen aspect of reality. Paul states "If in Christ we have hope in this life only, we are of all people most to be pitied" (1 Cor. 15:19). Paul is talking about the unseen aspect of reality rooted in God's promises and in which we place our hope. Those who cannot fathom placing their hope in the unseen aspect of reality reject Christianity, but not because they don't believe it to be true, but because they are afraid it might be true.

Our hearts point us to the transcendent realm of our existence because our hearts are made to want our transcendent Creator. But that's not all that supports the veracity of the Christian faith. While the Christian faith deals with the unseen, it is also backed by material facts—of the resurrection, of fulfilled prophecy, of transformed lives, and of the intricate and interdependent design of creation. Reality, therefore, best corresponds with the facts of the Christian faith. If you want truth, your best approach is to search the Scriptures and measure everything you hear against the Word of God. And the truth is, Jesus is coming back to gather His elect and judge the world. Will you be one of the gathered?

CHAPTER
SIX

ETERNAL VALUE

"But store up for yourselves treasures in heaven,
where moths and vermin do not destroy, and
where thieves do not break in and steal."

~Matthew 6:20, NIV

My three-year-old son loves to play with me. I love my three-year-old son, but I've never been very good at make believe. Around the clock I hear, "Come and build me a tower!" I'm always tempted to respond the "responsible" way: "After I do the dishes" or "I need to finish my work." All day long, his requests are relentless. Usually it takes me connecting with his sweet, hopeful stare to finally get down on my knees and build an "epic" train track or marble run. My heart swells as I experience his joy. I often wonder why I would ever want to miss out on quality time with any of my children while I have it.

I guess I'm not alone when it comes to mixing up my priorities. The Bible recounts the experience of sisters named

Mary and Martha. Martha welcomed Jesus into their home only to leave Him to attend to the "responsible" things to do. Her sister, Mary, however, sat at Jesus's feet and listened to his teaching. You may have been there with your siblings: you work while they play. It gets annoying. But Jesus clarified the issue, "Martha, Martha, you are anxious and troubled about many things, but one thing is necessary. Mary has chosen the good portion, which will not be taken away from her" (Luke 10:41-42).

The "good portion" is how we choose to spend our time *now* that has value for *eternity*. Mary chose the "good portion." Martha and I chose "many things." "Many things" have no eternal value, they erode and fade away; but *one* thing will never be taken away: Jesus. Jesus, as well as the spiritual fruit that comes from abiding in Him, *is* the *good portion*. I dare to say that no other book of the Bible highlights the urgency of making this choice than the book of Revelation. Revelation points a finger at what will happen if we *don't* choose the good portion of eternal value.

> The "good portion" is how we choose to spend our time *now* that has value for *eternity*.

When most people hear the term "the end times," they think of the last book of the Bible. Revelation tells the seamless story of redemptive history using apocalyptic imagery. Apocalyptic style of writing uses obscure images (that is, obscure to contemporary audiences) that draw on Old Testament motifs and symbols. In other words, most of the symbols in Revelation made sense to a first-century audience. When contemporary audiences use the correct interpretive tools, the apocalyptic imagery can make sense to us too.

The author of Revelation is the Apostle John, the former disciple of Jesus who also penned the Gospel of John as well as the Epistles of John. John used this apocalyptic imagery to record his visions about God's plan for the future, with special emphasis on how His plan ends. His plan ends with Jesus returning to gather His elect, but judge the world.

Christ's Second Coming will be stunning and climactic.[46] Patrick Johnstone says it this way: "Everything is heading towards a climax—both evil and good. It will be high tide at midnight. The darkness will increase at that midnight hour, but that will also be the high tide of the Church as she is readied for the Bridegroom."[47]

Luke recounts the Apostle Peter's observation when Jesus ascended into heaven—and the foretelling of His return.

---

46 Revelation deals with history past, present, and future. We glean from the past to help us live in our present as we prepare for the future events foretold therein. To properly interpret Revelation, we must look to its original era, culture, and language. We look to the New and Old Testaments to allow Scripture to interpret Scripture. I am relaying just a glimpse of the events prophesied to occur at the end of the Age. A more thorough examination of the time frame and events is warranted. This can be found throughout the Bible, but especially in Daniel, Ezekiel, Joel, Zechariah, Isaiah, Jeremiah, the Gospels, the Epistles, and cross-references within Revelation itself.

47 Patrick Johnstone, "Expecting a Harvest," in *Perspectives on the World Christian Movement: A Reader*, ed. Ralph D. Winter and Steven C. Hawthorne, 382–386 (Pasadena: William Carey Library, 2009), 384.

"And when he had said these things, as they were looking on, he was lifted up, and a cloud took him out of their sight. And while they were gazing into heaven as he went, behold, two men stood by them in white robes, and said, 'Men of Galilee, why do you stand looking into heaven? This Jesus, who was taken up from you into heaven, will come in the same way as you saw him go into heaven'" (Acts 1:9–11).

Christ's Second Coming (also known as His "glorious appearing") is undoubtedly the most anticipated event in world history because it marks the end of the world as we know it and the beginning of an eternity of rest with our Lord.

Remember, the Church Age is the era between Christ's first and second advents on earth. This era is the time we are living in right now. It is governed by the New Covenant of grace through faith in Jesus Christ as mediated by the Holy Spirit in the hearts of every believer. All of humanity (including you and me) who live at any time after Christ's resurrection but before His Second Coming live in the transition between the "already" and "not yet."

Here we are, living in the era of Christ's return, and we don't know when it will actually happen. Jesus warned that His Second Coming would be at an hour no one will expect. "Therefore you also must be ready, for the Son of Man is coming at an hour you do not expect" (Matt. 24:44). We haven't been given a timetable to chart how much time we have left. What do we do in the interim while we wait? A better question might be, what happens when you don't know when someone will return?

In a large family like ours, it's essential to divide and conquer. Everyone has duties assigned. Every once in a while I'll dole out an extra chore or two—usually when I'm away on an errand. What parent hasn't uttered these words, "Better have that done by the time I return . . ."? In order to gauge how urgently they should engage, my children usually ask a few questions like "Where are you going?" or "When are you coming back?"

But sometimes they forget to ask and I forget to tell. What are the chances they have finished their chores by the time I get home? Whether I'm gone five minutes or five hours, there is very little chance they would have completed the task. Inevitably they get distracted with their own interests until I surprise them by walking in the door and they scurry to get it all done.

So what is the majority of the world and even the church doing while they wait for Jesus's return? Striving to get rich, famous, and powerful. Little do they realize: they are being set up by Satan. It's a trap to lure well-intentioned people away from the nagging on their heart and toward their efforts to achieve. The temptation is real, it works, and it is presently working in the very lives of even those who call themselves Christians.

What does the Bible say about this source of distraction? One of the most prominent symbolisms used in Revelation for the counterfeit systems of the world is known therein as "Babylon." This includes the system in which we buy and sell; it may include an ecclesiastical body or system that distorts the Gospel. It definitely symbolizes worldly means of obtaining wealth and power.[48] Therefore, Babylon is understood to represent humanity's imitation source of security and purpose. Babylon was a real city in the ancient world. The literal city of Babylon is in present-day Iraq. How interesting the symbolic city that will be destroyed has also been a hub of religious and political turmoil in the Middle East—yesterday, today, and certainly tomorrow.

The author, John, describes symbolic Babylon as the "great prostitute who corrupted the earth with her immorality" (Rev. 19:2). How is this represented today? Perhaps the world's monetary system that prostitutes itself as a cheap substitute for a saving relationship with Jesus Christ. Religious systems, even "Christian" ones that require payments for penance or in return for salvation or favors from saints distort the truth of

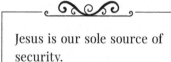

Jesus is our sole source of security.

Jesus being the only way to the Father. We are to remember that Jesus is our sole source of security, not any human or monetary sanctuary. He provides a living hope in the "already" for the

---

48   "Fallen, fallen is Babylon the great!
      She has become a dwelling place for demons,
      a haunt for every unclean spirit,
      a haunt for every unclean bird,
      a haunt for every unclean and detestable beast.
      For all nations have drunk
      the wine of the passion of her sexual immorality,
      and the kings of the earth have committed immorality with her,
      and the merchants of the earth have grown rich from the power of her
      luxurious living"
      (Rev. 18:2–3).

best that is our "not yet." We idolize Babylon when we exalt success, wealth, and idols of the heart above God.

Revelation, therefore, paints a vivid picture of the state of the world at the end of the Age. How will this play out? "Fallen, fallen is Babylon the great!" The world and all of its imitation offerings will collapse.

Think about it. The trigger for such an event could be seemingly innocuous at first and yet have a ripple effect that topples one after another like dominoes. Once the first domino in the marketplace falls, other cataclysmic events could follow due to deteriorating conditions. Before the world knows it, Babylon will have fallen.

What will happen to you when all the security you've amassed from money in the bank (or cryptocurrency) collapses, the housing market collapses, the Baltic Dry Index collapses, GDP collapses, or the religion you have trusted is exposed as corrupt? I pray if it happens in your lifetime, you take the losses in stride knowing you can't take them with you to eternity. I pray you accept the clarity about true faith through Jesus with humility rather than give into the temptation to dig your heels in the ground.

I have found, however, that many Christians respond to these warnings about the fate of the world in one of two ways: prepare to save their lives or prepare to save their souls. Prepping for disasters used to be something for those on the fringes of society. Now everyone is doing it. We feel a foreboding, and we want to be prepared in case of emergency.

Prepping isn't a bad thing unless it causes you to neglect the more important task of preparing your soul to accept the way, the truth, and the life. Jesus taught, "For whoever would save his life will lose it, but whoever loses his life for my sake will find it" (Matt. 16:25). In the event the Tribulation Period does begin in our lifetimes, losing our mortal lives will be the least of our concerns. Our faith will be tested. Preparing to last as long as possible in order to help others prepare their souls can be a noble use of any stockpile you may be tempted to amass.

What is of eternal value? The human soul. The most repeated instruction relating to the Second Coming of Jesus Christ is to make Him known to others. While Satan tempts people to a harvest of riches, God is preparing for a harvest of souls. Friends, the time is ripe for a worldwide revival. "I believe we are now in the time of the final ingathering before the end."[49] Today we have the technological capability to reach everyone with the Gospel, a condition precedent to a worldwide revival of souls.

Jesus says that the Gospel will be preached to all the nations before He returns (Matt. 24:14). Additionally, Isaiah 54 foretells of the Jews' abundant spiritual growth. "'Sing O barren one, who did not bear; break forth into singing and cry aloud, you who have not been in labor! For the children of the desolate one will be more than the children of her who is married,' says the Lord" (Isa. 54:1). Furthermore, in Ezekiel we learn that God will cause dry bones to live as He breathes spiritual life into them anew (Ezek. 37:1–14). The New Testament also foretells of a time when the original branch of the vine, the Jews, will

---

49   Johnstone, "Expecting a Harvest," 383.

believe, regain faith, and be grafted back into salvation. "For if you [Gentiles] were cut from what is by nature a wild olive tree, and grafted, contrary to nature, into a cultivated olive tree, how much more will these, the natural branches, be grafted back into their own olive tree" (Rom. 11:24). All of these Scriptures speak of restoration, new life, and revival for at least the Jewish people, if not all who would believe in the world.

Restoration, new life, and revival come as we focus on things of eternal value, not on the temptations of Babylon. "But

> Restoration, new life, and revival come as we focus on things of eternal value, not on the temptations of Babylon.

store up for yourselves treasures in heaven, where moths and vermin do not destroy, and where thieves do not break in and steal (Matt. 6:20, NIV). We each must honestly assess in whom or what we place our trust. Are we more worried about our financial security than our spiritual security? Do we busy ourselves with the "responsible" things to do and let the love and joys of life slip away? In the end, no amount of rationalization will change God's mind. You are either with Him or against Him; you either choose the good portion or you settle for the bad portion.

Today, ask God what in your life you may consciously or even unconsciously be putting above Him. If you have not yet confessed that Jesus is your Lord and Savior, you can do that now. Remember, every day is one day closer to the end of your opportunity for eternal salvation. Make the decision to invest in things of eternal value. Take up your cross every day in response to your belief in who Jesus is and what He did for you. Don't put it off—*today* is the day of salvation.

Dear Lord, thank you for your amazing grace that saved a sinner like me. I believe that you are the Son of God who rose from the dead so that I can have eternal life. I admit I have sought security in other things that will fade away. I now put my faith in you and your promises of eternal value. I commit to taking up my cross daily and living out my faith. Help me help advance the kingdom of God for your glory. In Jesus's name, Amen.

FAITHFUL TO FORGIVE

*"If we confess our sins, he is faithful and
just and will forgive us our sins and
cleanse us from all unrighteousness."*

~1 John 1:9

S haron was a beautiful girl. A life marred by abuse led
her to leveraging her looks for survival. By the time
Sharon turned twenty-two, she was the mistress of an
oil tycoon. Commitment didn't interest her. In her experience,
commitment led to rejection. Over the years, she leap-frogged
over the hearts of many men, causing several divorces.

Then, she met *him,* the love of her life. Suddenly, the rest
of the world disappeared. Instead of the Ritz, she relished
candlelight dinners. In place of diamonds, she chose handholds.
In lieu of jet planes, she now preferred walks in the park.
Commitment was a small sacrifice to make for true love.

Six months into their courtship, her partner was diagnosed
with cancer. Six month after that, he died. In her despair, she

believed his death was God's punishment for her reckless life choices. She devastated families, so He devastated hers. She was certain God could never forgive her selfishness.

You may not share the same story as Sharon, but you may harbor the same shame about your own decisions. Rest assured, God doesn't punish us in the age of grace. Our choices have natural consequences, yes. This world has disease and death, abuse and pain. If natural consequences terrify you, something in your past, even your present, may make you fear God's coming judgment. The thought of facing Jesus on the judgment throne at the end of your life may have you running to hide. Guilt and shame may threaten to hold you back from your future inheritance as a child of God. Your feelings of unworthiness may threaten to drown out any potential purpose for your life.

Are we ever too far gone for God? Is there a point of no return where God just can't or won't forgive?

Let me assure you, God loves you still. You were chained to your mistakes, but through Christ's blood, you are free. The chains are broken. You have permission to take back the gift of the present through God's forgiveness. "There is therefore now no condemnation for those who are in Christ Jesus" (Rom. 8:1). With Christ, your past no longer condemns you.

> You were chained to your mistakes, but through Christ's blood, you are free.

Have you heard the story of the two sons? One was an eternal optimist, the other a pessimist. Their parents tried in vain to help their sons find some middle ground to temper their extreme worldviews. One day, they decided to set up a disappointment for the optimist and a reward for the pessimist. "That will change them," the parents expressed.

"Boys," the parents called, "there's something for you in the barn!"

The excited duo rushed to see. The parents led the pessimist to where the pony stood, and led the optimist to the pony's manure. True to form, the pessimist cried, "Shucks! A pony!? That means I'll have to clean up poo!" The optimist, seeing only the poo said, "Wow! Look at all that poo! That means there must be a pony nearby!"

How you see your circumstances matters. Even in the worst of them, God provides a silver lining if we will look for it. We are sure to find it if we look with our whole heart. Finding it will change the quality of our reality.

When we see the "poo" in our lives as potential for God's glory, we are empowering our purpose in the middle of tribulation. Instead of anticipating lament and struggle, we anticipate a silver lining. We have a new perspective that anticipates the goodness of God that keeps us looking up, not down; forward, not backward.

I dare say we have all done things that Jesus died to erase from God's eyes. Memories, expectations, beliefs, problems, past behavior, past mistakes, and experiences with others all make up our past and pollute our memories. When we are young, we have little control over the events that help shape us.

But we are no longer children. We have the maturity and knowledge to equip ourselves to make the right choices. God's truth is the only reliable perspective to help us see where we are compared to where God needs us to be. God's wisdom gives us a new perspective. It gives us courage and comfort to move beyond our bad memories and into God's good promises. When you trade your dim lens for the clear lens of God, everything you see and experience in this life will change into something for which you can give thanks while you lift up your requests to Him. God's lens enables us to see ourselves as God sees us: forgiven, redeemed, purified, accepted, wanted, and loved.

A torrid or painful past has no grip on anyone except the enemy who wants to use it to condemn you. In fact Satan will condemn you for the very sin he tempted you into. The enemy doesn't want you to feel worthy of Christ's forgiveness. But know this: you are never too far-gone for Christ's love.

> God's lens enables us to see ourselves as God sees us: forgiven, redeemed, purified, accepted, wanted, and loved.

Just before Sodom and Gomorrah were about to be destroyed, the angel who saved Lot and his family warned them not to look back. Lot's wife disobeyed and looked back, so God turned her into a pillar of salt.[50] We do not benefit God's kingdom or ourselves when we look back at destruction when God promises life ahead.

As I was writing this chapter, a friend of mine called to share how much she has enjoyed reading through the chronological Bible. The stories of God's faithfulness with some

---

50 See Gen. 19:26, "But Lot's wife, behind him, looked back, and she became a pillar of salt."

of the most notorious biblical figures had given her great hope in her early walk with Christ. Rereading them now affirmed how important it was for her to know that Christ came to redeem the *lost*. My friend grieved over her past mistakes, but she did not dwell there. Instead, she dwelled on the goodness of God. "Sara," she said, "If God can forgive Paul, I know he can forgive me too."

> A torrid or painful past has no grip on anyone except the enemy who wants to use it to condemn you.

If you are unfamiliar with Paul, his conversion testimony is one to note. Formerly known as "Saul," Paul was a devout and religious Jew thoroughly trained in the law of his Jewish ancestors. Saul had authority, and he used it to ruthlessly persecute Christians. "But Saul was ravaging the church, and entering house after house, he dragged off men and women and committed them to prison" (Acts 8:3). Saul had an active role in the stoning of Stephen, the first Christian martyr of the church. "They cried out with a loud voice and stopped their ears and rushed together at him. Then they cast [Stephen] out of the city and stoned him. And the witnesses laid down their garments at the feet of a young man named *Saul*" (Acts 7:57-58, italics mine). Here is Paul's confession in his own words:

> "I myself was convinced that I ought to do many things in opposing the name of Jesus of Nazareth. And I did so in Jerusalem. I not only locked up many of the saints in prison after receiving authority from the chief priests,

but when they were put to death I cast my vote against them. And I punished them often in all the synagogues and tried to make them blaspheme, and in raging fury against them I persecuted them even to foreign cities" (Acts 26:9-11).

Despite these atrocities, Paul was not too far-gone for God. One day, as Saul walked toward Damascus, a light from heaven, brighter than the sun, shone around him and the people with whom he journeyed. They fell to the ground. A voice said to Saul:

"'Saul, Saul, why are you persecuting me? It is hard for you to kick against the goads.' And I said, 'Who are you, Lord?' And the Lord said, 'I am Jesus whom you are persecuting. But rise and stand upon your feet, for I have appeared to you for this purpose, to appoint you as a servant and witness to the things in which you have seen me and to those in which I will appear to you, delivering you from your people and from the Gentiles—to whom I am sending you to open their eyes, so that they may turn from darkness to light and from the power of Satan to God, that they may receive forgiveness of sins and a place among those who are sanctified by faith in me'" (Acts 26:14-18).

Jesus changed Saul's name to Paul to work on His behalf, taking the Good News of Jesus Christ to the Gentiles. In fact, Paul's enormous influence on the church continues to this day as he wrote the majority of the New Testament.

God is not in the business of shame, but He is in the business of redemption. God redeemed Saul (Paul) for a purpose, and He is willing to do the same for you. Your life is not an accident. You were made for a purpose. God will help you fulfill that purpose when you turn to Him, believe Jesus is His Son whom He raised from the dead, and, like Saul, endure persecution in this life to follow him.

There is only one perspective that matters, and that is the perspective of what is to come for those who have their lives hidden with God in Christ. We can leave the past behind knowing we have the glorious promise of an eternal future with Christ in heaven.

How do we approach God when we realize we want to be forgiven but don't think it's possible? There are three small steps we can take to position ourselves to receive God's gift of forgiveness: repent, forgive others, and receive.

◈ REPENT

The opening verse from 1 John speaks to a simple condition precedent to God's forgiveness—confession of our sins. God wants to forgive us, but He can't forgive what we don't recognize needs to be forgiven.

When we confess, we tell God that we admit what we did, said, or thought was wrong. When we commit to turning from these ways, we elevate our confession to repentance. Repentance is the key that unlocks the door to forgiveness by God.

We cannot possibly repent for every mistake we have made

or idle word we have spoken, so we admit that we are sinners who are bent on going our own way and satisfying our desires rather than pleasing God. We learn what pleases God and strive to live accordingly from that moment forward.

In fact, when Scripture speaks of salvation, it often uses the term "repentance" instead of salvation.

- "When they heard these things they fell silent. And they glorified God, saying, 'Then to the Gentiles also God has granted repentance that leads to life'" (Acts 11:18).
- "God may perhaps grant them repentance leading to a knowledge of the truth" (2 Tim. 2:25b).
- "Or do you presume on the riches of his kindness and forbearance and patience, not knowing that God's kindness is meant to lead you to repentance?" (Rom. 2:4).

As these Scriptures point out, repentance:

- "leads to" life and knowledge of the truth
- is "granted by" God
- is motivated by God's kindness, tolerance, and patience.

The good news about repentance: you relinquish retribution to Christ. Jesus willingly died to take the punishment for your repented sin. God wants you to be free from the consequences of your sin.

> Humbly repent to God and reap the eternal rewards of never-failing forgiveness from your Heavenly Father.

Free to serve Him in return. Free to reach your potential for His glory. Humbly repent to God and reap the eternal rewards of never-failing forgiveness from your Heavenly Father.

One of the great examples of repentance comes from King David. This man after God's own heart had a difficult time facing down temptation. David had faced many adversities, even being pursued by his father-in-law, King Saul, to be murdered. God delivered him from all danger unharmed. Yet, when he looked upon a woman named Bathsheba in a rooftop bath, he violated the laws of marriage and took her for himself. The result of their unholy union was a pregnancy. How David dealt with this consequence led him further down the road of sin. He had Bathsheba's husband, Uriah, "accidentally" killed in battle.[51]

In those days, God had prophets send messages to the people. The prophet Nathan was sent to give a message to King David, "Why have you despised the word of the LORD, to do what is evil in his sight? You have struck down Uriah the Hittite with the sword and have taken his wife to be your wife and have killed him with the sword of the Ammonites" (2 Sam. 12:9).

David could have responded in any number of ways. Thankfully, he repented. "David said to Nathan, 'I have sinned against the LORD" (2 Sam. 12:13(a)). And the Lord was faithful to forgive. "And Nathan said to David, "The LORD also has put away your sin; you shall not die" (2 Sam. 12:13(b)).

---

51 See 2 Samuel 11 for more details.

Psalm 51 recounts David's repentance:

> "'Have mercy on me, O God,
> according to your steadfast love;
> according to your abundant mercy
> blot out my transgressions.
> Wash me thoroughly from my iniquity,
> and cleanse me from my sin!
> For I know my transgressions,
> and my sin is ever before me.
> Against you, you only, have I sinned
> and done what is evil in your sight,
> so that you may be justified in your words
> and blameless in your judgment.
> Behold, I was brought forth in iniquity,
> and in sin did my mother conceive me.
> Behold, you delight in truth in the inward being,
> and you teach me wisdom in the secret heart"
> (Ps. 51:1-6).

King David's contrite heart can set the standard for our repentance as well. Repentance paved the way for God's forgiveness by removing barriers to God's purpose for David. Repentance opens the same path for those who humbly admit and turn from the areas in their life where they have disobeyed God.

◈ FORGIVE OTHERS

There was once a king who wanted to settle his accounts. A man owned him ten thousand dollars but could not pay, so the king ordered him to be sold along with his family. The man begged for mercy, so the king forgave him his entire debt. Then the forgiven man found someone who owned him one hundred dollars. This debtor pleaded for mercy, but instead of showing the next man the same mercy granted to him, the forgiven man put his debtor in prison.

> "Then his master summoned him and said to him, 'You wicked servant! I forgave you all that debt because you pleaded with me. And should not you have had mercy on your fellow servant, as I had mercy on you?' And in anger his master delivered him to the jailers, until he should pay all his debt. So also my Heavenly Father will do to every one of you, if you do not forgive your brother from your heart" (Matt. 18:32–35).

The king in this parable made the point that being forgiven by God is of a much greater debt than anyone owes us. We must pay the gift forward to show our true appreciation for the mercy our sovereign Lord showed to us. Have you ever thought why the Lord's Prayer includes this request: "forgive us our debts as we also have forgiven our debtors" (Matt. 6:12)? Scripture is clear, if we show no mercy, our heart is not truly humbled. The hatred that we conceal as justified anger is just another sin for which we need to be forgiven. And that sin will continue needing forgiveness until we eliminate that sin by forgiving those who have harmed us. "Be kind to one another, tenderhearted, forgiving one another, as God in Christ forgave you" (Eph. 4:32). "The Lord forgave you, so you must forgive others" (Col. 3:13, NLT).

The good news, forgiveness is a decision.

Forgiveness is not a good feeling about our perpetrator; it is not rekindling a relationship with them; and it is definitely not showing a weakness or giving up power. Forgiveness does not deny what happened, it releases us from the burden of what happened.

You don't have to feel it.

You don't have to rekindle a relationship.

You don't even have to forget.

Forgiveness is freedom and power to live according to the riches of God's mercy. Because we *choose* to forgive, we retain our power in Christ. We forgive so that our Heavenly Father can forgive us.

> Forgiveness is freedom and power to live according to the riches of God's mercy.

◈ RECEIVE

I've heard forgiveness termed a "miracle." But that may imply that it is rare. In contemporary lingo, "it's a miracle!" means something unexpected or a surprise. Forgiveness is not a miracle in that sense. Forgiveness is more like a gift. A gift is available to be received and it is available to be given; it is yours for the taking, or in the alternative, yours to reject.

When Jesus was gathering His disciples, He greeted Nathaniel with approval. Nathaniel, who had never met Jesus before, replied, "How do you know me?" Jesus answered, "'Before Philip called you, when you were under the fig tree, I saw you'" (John 1:48). Jesus's supernatural vision of Nathaniel earlier in the day immediately transformed Nathaniel's heart into a follower of Jesus. Nathaniel responded to Jesus's invitation to come and see because Jesus first saw (and accepted) Nathaniel.

Jesus sees you too. And He accepts your scars, mistakes, and all. Jesus knows more about us than we can possibly imagine— everything. You cannot surprise God. You also cannot hide from God. He already sees you, He already knows everything about you, and He loves you still.

When God looks at a believer—someone who has put his or her faith in Jesus Christ—He sees Jesus. That's the "rosy" part of the glasses. So don't be surprised when you continue to make mistakes even after you repent and accept Jesus as your Lord and Savior. God's desire is that you stay faithful in the face of adversity and trial. But God will use these experiences to grow your endurance through difficult experiences. What matters is that you have a contrite heart willing to repent as your journey through temptations and trials.

Today, the doors to your jail cell are wide open! You are free to walk out. But will you?

God gives us opportunities to receive His forgiveness because His view of us is not formed by our mistakes. God sees our glorified version. God knows what we are able to *be*. That is the version God embraces now, even while we are still broken and breaking. He's waiting patiently for us to see ourselves through His rosy-colored glasses and embrace our potential in Him. When we repent, forgive, and receive, God remembers our past no more. "As far as the east is from the west, so far has he removed our transgressions from us" (Ps. 103:12, NIV).

You can receive God's forgiveness today by taking one small step into a new life. God's forgiveness frees you from your thoughts and feelings of guilt and shame, our past, and the power of darkness. Today, the doors to your jail cell are wide open! You are free to walk out.

But will you?

Heavenly Father, help me keep my perspective on you and not on my past circumstances. These past experiences and problems did not honor you, whether due to my choices or the choices of someone else. But today is a gift. I can honor you today. Show me how. Help me hide your Word in my heart so I can be prepared when the lies try to bring me down. I realize this is one of the very first steps I must make to change my perspective, change my life, and change my eternity. Thank you for your love. In Jesus's name, Amen.

ANTICIPATION IN TRIBULATION

"Set your minds on things that are above, not on things that are on earth. For you have died, and your life is hidden with Christ in God. When Christ who is your life appears, then you also will appear with him in glory."

~Colossians 3:2–4

The desire to experience an intimate love connection strikes a chord in every human heart. No matter how wonderful and fulfilling our relationships may be, no human relationship will ever fully satisfy our need for true intimacy. The blessing of human intimacy merely shadows the true intimacy we will experience in relationship with our Savior, Jesus Christ. Marriage is a sacred institution

> The blessing of human intimacy merely shadows the true intimacy we will experience in relationship with our Savior, Jesus Christ.

to God for this very reason. In order to illustrate such intimacy, God uses the image of marriage— the ultimate form of human attachment—as an expression of the deep intimacy for which our souls were made.

Who doesn't look forward to a wedding? Near the end of the Tribulation Period, the Lamb of God and the Bride of Christ are getting married. For the Bride and Christ, this has come to be known as the Marriage Supper of the Lamb. The Marriage Supper of the Lamb depicts the deep love Christ has for His Bride when they are reunited in eternal, holy matrimony. Believers can look forward to this wedding celebration with all their hearts.

Just like any wedding, the ceremony is followed up with a celebratory meal. According to John MacArthur, Hebrew weddings consisted of three phases: the betrothal, presentation, and ceremony. He too believes that the marriage supper signifies the end of the marriage ceremony.[52]

In God's wedding portrayal, the Bridegroom is the Lamb of God, a symbol for Jesus Christ. "Behold, the Lamb of God, who takes away the sin of the world!" (John 1:29).[53] This symbol is taken from Old Testament imagery of the sin offering as well as the Passover, which required the annual sacrifice of

---

52 John MacArthur, *Revelation: A Christian's Ultimate Victory* (Nashville: Thomas Nelson, 2007), 117.

53 See also Isa. 53:7, Rev. 5:6.

an unblemished lamb.[54] Passover foreshadowed the voluntary sacrifice of unblemished (sinless) Jesus for the sins of the world.[55]

The Bride represents the church of believers. Paul wrote about the marriage of Christ to the church. "For I feel a divine jealousy for you, since I betrothed you to one husband, to present you as a pure virgin to Christ" (2 Cor. 11:2). To the church at Ephesus, Paul compares the role of the husband and wife to Christ's relationship with the church. "This mystery is profound, and I am saying that it refers to Christ and the church." (Eph. 5:32).

The Marriage Supper of the Lamb is a celebration for those who did not allow their faith in Jesus to "fall asleep" during their lifetime. The celebration is only awarded to those who persevere through hardship, suffering, and persecution and remain faithful to Jesus—even unto death.

God's use of "marriage" symbolizes more than just a celebration. Marriage is the lifetime union of one man and one woman. To be married means to join together as one flesh.

> The Marriage Supper of the Lamb is a celebration for those who did not allow their faith in Jesus to "fall asleep" during their lifetime.

What happens when a man and a woman get married? They forsake all other romantic relationships, even familial ones, to commit to their spouse. Their entire lives change to live and submit to each other every day for the rest of their lives. Other than God, spouses are to

---

54   See Leviticus 4:32–35 and Exodus 12:3–27.

55   See 1 Peter 1:19.

place each other above every other earthly relationship. In like manner, believers are to forsake the world and commit to their relationship with Christ. The church stands in stark contrast to the world for this reason. As one author wrote, "You did not accept Jesus's invitation if your life didn't change like a new bride's does when she gets married. You are married to Jesus when you live with him every day, forsaking all others, and seeking to submit to him in everything."[56]

When we accept Jesus, we do more than accept Jesus for who He is. Our entire lives will transform as a result of our heart's transformation. The change may not be immediate and drastic (although it can be), but it will be persistent as God convicts your heart to accept the things that please Him and reject the things that do not please Him. We are called to stay faithful to our Bridegroom, Jesus, no matter what our flesh wants to do.

Do you want to do accept Jesus and be transformed by the renewal of you mind and heart? Are you currently living in violation of God-defined marriage? It is not too late to repent and change course. God will forgive us if we confess and turn from our sin.

How do believers access the Marriage Supper of the Lamb? This wedding feast is another anticipated event for believers.

---

56   Mark Ballenger, "Is it Biblical to Just "Accept Jesus into Your Heart" to be Saved? What to Say When Evangelizing," *AGW The Teaching Ministry of Mark Ballenger*, applygodsword.com, Oct. 15, 2015, accessed October 22, 2020, https://applygodsword.com/is-it-biblical-to-just-accept-jesus-into-your-heart-to-be-saved/.

◈ RAPTURE

Believers throughout the Church Age who have repented of their sin, accepted Jesus Christ as their Lord and Savior, and stayed faithful to Jesus will be taken to heaven to meet Jesus in the air and dine with Him at the Marriage Supper of the Lamb. "In a moment, in the twinkling of an eye, at the last trumpet. For the trumpet will sound, and the dead will be raised imperishable, and we shall be changed" (1 Cor. 15:52). This event is echoed to the Thessalonian church:

> "For the Lord himself will descend from heaven with a cry of command, with the voice of an archangel, and with the sound of the trumpet of God. And the dead in Christ will rise first. Then we who are alive, who are left, will be caught up together with them in the clouds to meet the Lord in the air, and so we will always be with the Lord" (1 Thess. 4:16–17).

Both believers who have died, as well as believers who are alive, will meet Jesus in the air in what is known as the "Rapture." The Rapture happens in "the twinkling of an eye" because we don't know the exact day and time that He will return. Thus, we will either be taken (or left behind) by surprise. "Then two men will be in the field; one will be taken and one left. Two women will be grinding at the mill; one will be taken and one left" (Matt. 24:40–41).

There are many theories on the timing of the Rapture. Some believe it will happen before the Tribulation Period (pretrib), some believe it will happen some time in the middle of the Tribulation Period (midtrib), and others believe it will occur after the judgments unleashed during the Tribulation Period (posttrib). Thus, depending on the timing of the Rapture, believers could experience this time of tribulation too.

Needless to say, anyone left on earth will be present for the Great Tribulation. Revelation explains the terrible judgments that God doles out on the world during this time. As mentioned, this period of unmatched distress will last seven years. These seven years will be split into two halves, with the second half being considerably worse.

Believers, pray we are raptured before any of these plagues take place. As mentioned earlier, even if we are present on earth, we can be assured it is temporary suffering. We have a glorious wedding feast to attend—not to mention the other wonderful blessings that await us on the other side of the Church Age. We can approach the end of our lives or the end of the Church Age with confidence.

Where do we get this confidence? Christian confidence comes from a *knowing* faith; that is, of having an *assurance* of things hoped for and a *conviction* of things not seen (Heb. 11:1). Christian faith is not blind; it is founded on reason and based in evidential, experiential, and rational truth. Jesus would not have summed up the Old Testament Law as loving Him with all of one's heart, soul, and *mind* if He didn't allow the use of these faculties to support our

We can approach the end of our lives or the end of the Church Age with confidence.

faith. When we engage our intellect to follow God, confidence in our faith grows in proportion to the confirmation of our intellectual pursuit. God's word will not return void (Isa. 55:11). As our confidence in the integrity of God's promises grows (especially that the best is yet to come), our fear of circumstances diminishes.

In the nineteenth-century, the Soviet Union came close to eradicating religion within its borders. Once an orthodox Christian nation, the threat of the church's political power triggered the government's indignation.[57] Atheism became the faith of post-Christian Russia. Atheism does not account for something more, let alone better, after this life. When one dies, they cease to exist. This ideology relegates all of one's pleasure to this life. There is no hope in anything to come. As a result, people question any cause, no matter how noble, that asks them to willingly sacrifice their ultimate gratification—their life.

Perhaps that's why during World War II that millions of Soviet troops either surrendered or allowed themselves to be captured. Joseph Stalin issued Order No. 270, labeling them traitors to be executed if they ever returned to the motherland. According to Evan Andrews, Order No. 227, better known as the "Not One Step Backward!" raised the bar by decreeing that cowards were to be "liquidated on the spot."[58]

57 Gene Zubovich, "Russian's Journey from Orthodoxy to Atheism and Back Again," October 16, 2018, *Religion & Politics: Fit for Polite Company*, accessed October 26, 2020, https://religionandpolitics.org/2018/10/16/russias-journey-from-orthodoxy-to-atheism-and-back-again/.

58 Evan Andrews, "8 Things You Should Know About WWII's Eastern Front: Explore eight facts about brutal and often overlooked Russian front of

Contrast this with the American troops from a culture steeped in Judeo-Christian values. Millions volunteered for service and fought to preserve the noble cause of freedom. They knew freedom was a God-given privilege to do what they ought, which for most was to stay faithful to Christ even unto death. In their eyes, the ultimate demonstration of faithfulness was laying down of one's life for another. Although not everyone subscribed to a Judeo-Christian worldview, by-and-large, the American culture did. It operated on the premise that this life is not the end of the road.

Today, we could be considered a post-Christian nation and world. Many in our society are also wondering why they would want to subscribe to any belief system that involves the loss of their lives through the events foretold in Revelation or elsewhere. They don't want to forfeit their one and only pleasure—this life and its pursuits.

It is imperative to understand that we have only our limited time on earth to make the most important decision—live for the day or live for the Promise. Whatever we choose to believe, our beliefs have consequences. Remember, when God decides to dispatch Jesus to gather His elect for the Marriage Supper of the Lamb, the time for grace will be over. There are no

> Remember, when God decides to dispatch Jesus to gather His elect for the Marriage Supper of the Lamb, the time for grace will be over. There are no second chances.

WWII," Jan. 21, 2020, *History*, accessed October 26, 2020, https://www.history.com/news/8-things-you-should-know-about-wwiis-eastern-front.

second chances. Only those clothed in pure white linen from having their sins washed in the blood of Christ can be invited. The doors to the feast will be shut and locked forever if you are late, sleeping, or spiritually unprepared when Christ comes back for His Bride.

Don't you want to celebrate your salvation at the Marriage Summer of the Lamb?

Heavenly Father, the anticipation of Christ's return makes me examine my own heart. Cleanse me, Lord, of all unrighteousness. I want to be present at the Marriage Supper of the Lamb. Calm my fears about the unknown. Help me rest in your trustworthy holiness. I repent of my idle words, my judgments, my anger, and my strife. You are my comfort and with you I can do all things, including harness my self-control to lead a life pleasing to you. In Jesus's name, Amen.

TWO MORE ERAS TO COME

*"And he seized the dragon, that ancient serpent, who
is the devil and Satan, and bound him for a thousand
years, and threw him into the pit, and shut it and sealed
it over him, so that he might not deceive the nations
any longer, until the thousand years were ended.
After that he must be released for a little while."*

~Revelation 20:2–3

I t just keeps getting better. There's more to God's story. Revelation gives imagery to the fulfillment of the age-old prophecies foretelling Christ's return to render justice to His enemies. Who are Christ's enemies? Christ's enemies reject His free offer of grace. They refuse His voluntary ransom payment for their very souls. It's important to note that the designation of "enemy" is one

> Despite His innocence, Christ did all the work, took all the heat, and paid the full price for *our* guilt.

we willingly take on by choice. *We* reject Jesus, He does not reject us. Despite His innocence, Christ did all the work, took all the heat, and paid the full price for *our* guilt.

The next two eras are for Christ's heirs—those who love Him! In the first of the two eras, everything is not yet made entirely new. Scripture teaches that there will not be an entirely new heaven and earth until after Satan has been bound for one thousand years.

◈ THE MILLENNIUM

After Christ returns to earth at the end of the Church Age at some time toward the end of the Great Tribulation period, He will defeat the False Prophet and the Beast.[59] The Dragon (Satan) will be bound only for a period of one thousand years. This era is referred to as "The Millennium."

> "And he seized the dragon, that ancient serpent, who is the devil and Satan, and bound him for a thousand years, and threw him into the pit, and shut it and sealed it over him, so that he might not deceive the nations any longer, until the thousand years were ended. After that he must be released for a little while" (Rev. 20:2–3).

With Satan bound, he will not be prowling around looking for someone to devour.[60] Did you know that we all have sin in

---

59 Revelation 19:20.

60 "Be sober-minded; be watchful. Your adversary the devil prowls around like a roaring lion, seeking someone to devour" (1 Peter 5:8).

our hearts, but we act on it when tempted by the world, our flesh, or the devil?

> "Let no one say when he is tempted, 'I am being tempted by God,' for God cannot be tempted with evil, and he himself tempts no one. But each person is tempted when he is lured and enticed by his own desire. Then desire when it has conceived gives birth to sin, and sin when it is fully grown brings forth death" (Jas. 1:13–15).

Without temptation from the devil, the Millennium will be a blessed era of unprecedented fairness, love, mercy, and grace. A select people will populate and reign on the earth during the Millennium.

> "Then I saw thrones, and seated on them were those to whom the authority to judge was committed. Also I saw the souls of those who had been beheaded for the testimony of Jesus and for the word of God, and those who had not worshiped the beast or its image and had not received its mark on their foreheads or their hand. They came to life and reigned with Christ for a thousand years" (Rev. 20:4).

Very important: There is a distinguishing feature of believers present during the Millennium. They do NOT take a mark to buy and sell on their right hand or forehead that will be required during the Tribulation Period, as specific in the Scripture above. The specific details provided in Revelation say, however, that the mark will be placed in the hand or forehead.

It will be required to buy and sell in the marketplace and has been dubbed the Mark of the Beast. The Bible warns not to take this mark because it is the equivalent to being branded for Satan's possession.

> "Also it causes all, both small and great, both rich and poor, both free and slave, to be marked on the right hand or the forehead, so that no one can buy or sell unless he has the mark, that is, *the name of the beast or the number of its name*" (Rev. 13:16–17, emphasis added).

Think about what this means. Do you like going to the movies? You'll need this mark. Do you need to buy groceries for yourself and your children? You'll need this mark. Do you want to travel, buy gas, and purchase plane tickets? You'll need this mark. How about paying taxes to avoid having your property repossessed or to avoid going to jail? You'll need this mark.

When the Bible says the Mark of the Beast is required to buy and sell, is placed in the hand and/or the forehead, and is the number 666, what will that look like in real life? Well, we don't know exactly, but with all the technology that has come about so quickly, we must use wisdom. I have faith believers will recognize the mark when they see it.

Recently, there has been some clamor about a new technology called Human Implantable Quantum Dot Microneedle Vaccination Delivery System.[61] It has been noted

---

61 "Quantum Dots Deliver Vaccines and Invisibly Encode Vaccination History in Skin" Genengnews.com, December 19, 2019, accessed October 16, 2020, https://www.genengnews.com/topics/drug-discovery/

that in order for the delivery system to work, it uses an enzyme called *Luciferase* Enzyme. There is also a patent application filed by a related entity titled "Cryptocurrency System Using Body Activity Data."[62]

It is not unforeseeable that the "powers that be" could require something like these technologies to minimize the risk of participating in the marketplace. It is not inconceivable that we could be desensitized into accepting something like a microchip to make buying and selling "safer" and more "convenient."

Many have extolled the virtues of the embeddable microchip: it supposedly lessens the opportunity for crime, eliminates the need for keys, enables easy access to personal health information, etc. In addition, it eliminates "dirty" and inconvenient cash, checks, and credit cards. One satirical rationale for the microchip nearly twenty years ago read:

> "One hundred and one uses for your personal implanted microchip. So why not take the chip and join our 'New World Order society'? Because we love you. . . . .Don't be a rebel or dissident to this grand plan to bring about global, national, social, and individual harmony and well-being. Because we love you. . . . Be a good little citizen

---

quantum-dots-deliver-vaccines-and-invisibly-encode-vaccination-history-in-skin/.

62   The abstract of the patent states in part, "Human body activity with a task provided to a user may be used in a mining process of a cryptocurrency system." The application includes wearable devises and does not mention a microchip explicitly. At this time of writing, the patent had not been awarded.

in our 'brave new world.' Because we love you. .
. . And, if you refuse to take the mark, then you
would be showing that you are unproductive
and a rebel to our new society and we won't like
that. Because we love you. . . .'[63]

If you think this is far-fetched, you need only turn on
the radio, open the Internet, or watch the news to notice the
proliferation of the idea. People in Sweden accept embedding
microchips in their skin to track health and purchases.[64] Even
companies in the United States allow their employees to use
such technology.[65]

According to the Children's Health Defense, U.S. military
personnel will be the first subjects for implanted biosensor
trials. The proposed intent is to optimize health and early
detection for disease outbreak using bio-integrated sensors.[66]

---

63 Anonymous, "Carl Sanders, Inventor of the Microchip," *Taddlecreek. com*, Christmas 2002, No. 9, accessed October 9, 2020, https://www. taddlecreekmag.com/the-testimony-of-carl-sanders-inventor-of-the-microchip?fbclid=IwAR0rRcW8VGwHChWUmYgYpXsTyGfVtpFR8 mdql_NzYjsi-Gf3tN7ZGl5rBmc.

64 Maddy Savage, "Thousands of Swedes Are Inserting Microchips Under Their Skin," October 22, 2018, *npr.org*, accessed October 9, 2020, https:// www.npr.org/2018/10/22/658808705/thousands-of-swedes-are-inserting-microchips-under-their-skin#:~:text=In%20Sweden%2C%20a%20 country%20rich, their%20hands%20against%20digital%20readers.

65 Jeff Baenen, "Wisconsin company holds 'chip party' to microchip workers," August 2, 2017, accessed October 9, 2020, https://www.chicagotribune. com/business/blue-sky/ct-wisconsin-company-microchips-workers-20170801-story.html.

66 Pam Long, "Microchips, Nanotechnology and Implanted Biosensors: The New Normal?" *Childrenshealthdefense.org*, accessed October 9, 2020, https://childrenshealthdefense.org/child-health-topics/

Read what the Children's Health Defense warns about the implanted biosensor technology:

> "The SARS-CoV-2 vaccine plans to incorporate this technology and there is no information on how the technology could be removed, if at all. 'Tiny biosensors that become one with the body' could imply a lifetime commitment."[67]

There is also a program known as ID2020, which advocates for the digital identification of people.[68] According to their website:

> "Identity is vital for political, economic, and social opportunity. But systems of identification are archaic, insecure, lack adequate privacy protection, and for over a billion people, inaccessible. Digital identify is being defined now—and we need to get it right."[69]

What's the big deal? What we are seeing right now is a convergence of factors we have never seen before. We have a microchip specifically designed for placement in the hand and/or the forehead.[70] We have restrictions to participate in the marketplace. We have reason to vaccinate to protect ourselves

---

military-vaccines/microchips-nanotechnology-and-implanted-biosensors-the-new-normal/?fbclid=lwAR0H6KDe-zLRuuQ_buJ36S-dwrcTel717VJ_LWRAj5y-g03KmZ4thHA38VM.

67   Pam Long, "Microchips, Nanotechnology and Implanted Biosensors."

68   "We Need to Get Digital ID Right," ID2020, https://id2020.org/.

69   "We Need to Get Digital ID Right."

70   Anonymous, "Carl Sanders."

and others. We have reason to want others to also be vaccinated before reengaging in public activities. We have programs advocating for digital identification. We are experiencing coin shortages and a rise of cryptocurrencies, moving us toward a cashless society for which an embeddable digital means for buying and selling might help facilitate.

If you think a mark required to buy and sell is unlikely to be mandated, consider this. I recently listened to a conservative financial advisor who opened his radio program by praising the virtues of a Covid vaccine for its potential to put the economy back in business. While he did not believe anyone should be *required* to get a vaccine, he does believe that if anyone *wants* to participate in the marketplace, the vaccine should be the price of admission. According to this host, anyone who wants to go to the movies, fly on a plane, buy groceries, etc. should have to be a "card-carrying" vaccine taker.

So what are we to do? We are to research, confirm, and prepare. Remember, it takes the convergence of at least three telltale factors to fulfill the qualifications of the mark: placed in hand and/or forehead, required to buy and sell, and associated with the number of a man: 666. A vaccine alone would not qualify. No matter what, we are to stay faithful to our Lord, Jesus Christ, even if that means suffering for not being able to buy and sell.

> So what are we to do? We are to research, confirm, and prepare.

"Here is a call for the endurance of the saints, those who keep the commandments of God and

their faith in Jesus. And I heard a voice from
heaven saying, 'Write this: Blessed are the dead
who die in the Lord from now on.' 'Blessed
indeed,' says the Spirit, 'that they may rest from
their labors, for their deeds follow them!'" (Rev.
14:12–13).

Some people want to alleviate worry by subscribing to
the pre-trib or mid-trib Rapture timing theory. However, just
because someone subscribes to the pre-trib or mid-trib Rapture,
does not make it a reality. No matter what position we subscribe
to, we have to consider the *possibility* that we are here for the
time that the Mark of the Beast is rolled out. We all need to
be concerned because we do not know. Studying Revelation,
there are a lot of unknowns but in the midst of the unknowns,
we still have God's guidance: through His Word (i.e. all the
prophecies about the future as well as about God's character)
and through His Holy Spirit strengthening us. In the event
Christians are around when the Mark of the Beast is mandated,
we must make a decision, and that decision calls for wisdom
and understanding (Rev. 13:18).

Those sealed by the Holy Spirit are unlikely to unknowingly
take this mark. Believers, ask for godly wisdom to discern. If
during your lifetime such a mark is required, do not take it
or else you will not be present during the Millennium, which
means you did not make it past the terrible times at the end of
the Church Age and will not have access to heaven.

If you *do* make it to the Millennium, you will be blessed for
it. In the Millennium, spiritual Israel's Messiah will reign on

earth as King of kings and Lord of lords for one thousand years of unprecedented peace on earth.

> "On that day his feet shall stand on the Mount of Olives that lies before Jerusalem on the east, and the Mount of Olives shall be split in two from east to west by a very wide valley, so that one half of the Mount shall move northward, and the other half southward" (Zech. 14:4).

We will once again have Christ on earth, yet this time, with perfect leadership and without the Antichrist spirit, the false prophet, or the Dragon (Satan) to tempt people into sin. Peace will blanket the land. Even the animals will get along.

> "The wolf shall dwell with the lamb,
> and the leopard shall lie down with the young goat,
> and the calf and the lion and the fattened calf together;
> and a little child shall lead them.
> The cow and the bear shall graze;
> their young shall lie down together;
> and the lion shall eat straw like the ox.
> The nursing child shall play over the hole of the cobra,
> and the weaned child shall put his hand on the adder's den.
> They shall not hurt or destroy
> in all my holy mountain;
> for the earth shall be full of the knowledge of the LORD
> as the waters cover the sea" (Isa. 11:6–9).

Never before on earth, aside from the Garden of Eden, will every created thing live in such harmony. Jesus, as the perfect, holy ruler, makes this possible.

◈ FINAL DIMENSION: THE NEW JERUSALEM

The final era in God's overarching plan of redemption is the new Jerusalem, where all things will be made new.

> "Then I saw a new heaven and a new earth, for the first heaven and the first earth had passed away, and the sea was no more. And I saw the holy city, new Jerusalem, coming down out of heaven from God, prepared as a bride adorned for her husband. And I heard a loud voice from the throne saying, 'Behold, the dwelling place of God is with man. He will dwell with them, and they will be his people, and God himself will be with them as their God. He will wipe away every tear from their eyes, and death shall be no more, neither shall there be mourning, nor crying, nor pain anymore, for the former things have passed away'" (Rev. 21:1–4).

At the end of the Millennium, Satan is loosed and tempts people into warring against Jesus. The outcome, however, has already been written. It is not even a competition. Jesus Christ defeats Satan and his cohorts. Satan is bound permanently, to be tortured continually for eternity.

> "And the devil who had deceived them was thrown into the lake of fire and sulfur where the beast and the false prophet were, and they will be tormented day and night forever and ever" (Rev. 20:10).

Sin, which once separated us from God, has been fully

recompensed through God's perfect justice, leaving nothing unclean to inhabit the new heaven and new earth. God's perfected children will spend their eternity dwelling with Him in a paradise of peace and love. The living hope embedded in the hearts of every believer is brought to fruition in the new Jerusalem. All of what God wanted for us, and all that humanity desired to experience from the beginning of time can now be fully realized.

You may ask how the new Jerusalem will differ (or not) from heaven. Verse 2 from the Scripture above states that the holy city, new Jerusalem, *comes down out of heaven* from God. The new Jerusalem is a distinct place from heaven, but contains all of heaven and, therefore, offers nothing less than heaven, and perhaps offers even more. Currently, heaven has to be separated from earth because earth operates according to time and contains not only sin, but also the devil and his demons to tempt the sin out of people. Heaven, on the other hand, contains nothing unclean and does not operate according to time.

After Satan is condemned to the eternal fire at the end of the Millennium, the old earth and heavens pass away. Even the sea is no more. At this time, heaven can "come down" and occupy or fill this space because nothing evil is there to taint it anymore. The new Jerusalem, therefore, consists of the place of our final, eternal existence, replacing all things old, corrupted, and decaying. For the purposes of this book, "heaven" and "new Jerusalem" can be used interchangeably to indicate the perfect, eternal abode available for believers to bask in the glory of God's presence—the best.

This final era is eternal. It never ends. This picture of eternal paradise may prompt the question of who will share such experience? Unfortunately, not everyone. The fact is, God gave us free will to accept or reject His free gift of salvation. "And calling the crowd to him with his disciples, he said to them, 'If anyone would come after me, let him deny himself and take up his cross and follow me'" (Mark 8:34). God won't force us to accept Him—He'll honor our decision. His love and desire for a relationship with us will never falter. The Apostle Paul explains:

> "The saying is trustworthy, for: If we have died with him, we will also live with him; if we endure, we will also reign with him; if we deny him, he also will deny us; if we are faithless, he remains faithful—for he cannot deny himself" (2 Tim. 2:11–13).

Where do those who do not follow Jesus go? There *is* an eternal home for people who choose not to follow Christ as their Savior. They will experience what Revelation calls "the second death." "Then Death and Hades were thrown into the lake of fire. This is the second death, the lake of fire. And if anyone's name was not found written in the book of life, he was thrown into the lake of fire" (Rev. 20:14–15).

Those who experience the second death are judged at what is called the "Great White Throne Judgment":

> "And I saw the dead, great and small, standing before the throne, and books were opened. Then another book was opened, which is the book

of life. And the dead were judged by what was written in the books, according to what they had done. And the sea gave up the dead who were in it, Death and Hades gave up the dead who were in them, and they were judged, each one of them, according to what they had done" (Rev. 20:12–13).

Many atheists believe that when humans die, they cease to exist. At death, their worst prospect is that they will experience nothing more; no sorrow, no joy—nothing. For nonbelievers, this view is preferable to the Bible's truth that there is a place of eternal suffering for those who forsake God.

The truth is, we are eternal beings and, therefore, cannot cease to exist. Genesis 1:27 states that God made man in His own image. As we are made in our eternal God's image, we are eternal beings. Matthew 25:46 explains that the wicked will go away into *eternal* punishment, but the righteous unto *eternal* life.

While our physical bodies may turn to dust upon the first death, our souls remain to be resurrected either (1) to eternal life with God in glorified bodies or (2) to the second death in eternal absence of God. Thus, the second death doesn't render a person's body extinct, but rather relegates the body to an eternal state in the lake that burns with fire and sulfur.

> "But as for the cowardly, the faithless, the detestable, as for murderers, the sexually immoral, sorcerers, idolaters, and all liars, their portion will be in the lake that burns

with fire and sulfur, which is the second death"
(Rev. 21:8).

If this seems harsh, we remember that Scripture tells us that
God wants not one to perish, but rather all to come to repentance
and have eternal life with Him (2 Pet. 3:9). God is patient and
faithful. He endures centuries of rejection to allow everyone the
opportunity to accept His free gift of grace. Despite humanity's
faithlessness, God will
remain faithful to His
Word. God never
breaks a promise, for
to do so would violate

> Despite humanity's faithlessness,
> God will remain faithful to His
> Word.

the essence of His holy character. "If we are faithless, he remains
faithful—for He cannot deny Himself" (2 Tim. 2:13). In Psalms,
God emphasizes: "I will not violate my covenant or alter the
word that went forth from my lips. Once for all I have sworn by
my holiness; I will not lie to David" (89:34-35).

Do you trust God? Or do you trust humanity? Open your
Bible and read about God's unique holiness that differentiates
and exalts His authority, knowledge, power, and goodness
above all of humanity. In the end, the world will exalt humanity
as sovereign rather than God. People will trust what humanity
knows and can discover above the unchanging truths of the
Bible. It will not end well for them.

This lifetime is your last chance to commit to Jesus. He
sacrificed so you could have eternal life. Avoid the second
death; repent and accept Jesus as your Lord and Savior today.

Dear Lord, I want to avoid the second death. I repent of all my sin. I thank you for dying so that I can call on your name, turn from my sin, and be forgiven. I believe you are the Son of God who conquered death. Give me wisdom to discern the Mark of the Beast if it is required during my lifetime. I pray believers will be raptured, but just in case, I would rather suffer for not taking the Mark than take it and suffer for eternity. Thank you for your faithfulness. In Jesus's name, Amen.

THE BEST: GOD'S HOLINESS REQUIRES IT AND HIS GRACE, JUSTICE, AND HOPE ENSURE IT

"And one called to another and said: "Holy, holy, holy is the Lord of hosts; the whole earth is full of his glory!"

~Isaiah 6:3

The benefit of getting a glimpse of God's plan far exceeds simply knowing the sequence of future events. The benefit amounts to learning about the character of the One who authored such plan. Why? Because the "best" is only as good as the one behind the promise.

I can promise to give you the best, but would you trust me? You may look at my past actions to see if I keep to my promises.

You may examine my influence and power to see if I am capable and have the resources to follow through. You may even interview others who have had experience with me to verify my reliability. Similarly, when deciding whether to trust the one in charge of our eternity, we ask if we can trust this "holy Lord of hosts?"

> The benefit amounts to learning about the character of the One who authored such plan.

"Cross my heart and hope to die, stick a needle in my eye." Who among us has not recited this oath? There seems to be a point in everyone's childhood when the risk of being burned by yet another promisor left us reeling for a remedy—a means of getting assurance that our buddy would uphold his or her end of the bargain. Each time our gullibility was exposed by trusting the untrustworthy, we dug our heels in a little more, looking for something that would protect us from being in that vulnerable position again.

Alas, this obscure pledge seemed to provide the perfect remedy. Little attention was likely paid to the gruesome threat of death and a literal needle in our eye. We saw it for what it was—welcome leverage where any promise requiring such enforcement probably had little backing by a responsible adult anyway. We never really intended to follow through. The irony.

If we do not even intend to follow through, how likely is it that the next guy would be any better than us? What makes one promisor more trustworthy than the next?

If humans set the standard of trustworthiness, then no wonder we question promisors. People change their minds by the hour, minute—even second. We all know how our trust erodes when the person on whom we rely flakes out on his or her promises. Thank goodness that God does not conform to the standard of fickle human nature. Scripture declares, "Jesus Christ is the same yesterday and today and forever" (Heb. 13:8). This matters. God is different than humans. Unlike us, He never wavers; never changes; never backs out. We can trust Him like we can trust no one else.

Thus, *how* the end time events play out is less important than *why* they play out. Unpacking the *why* starts with understanding the *who*. If we want to trust that the best is yet to come, we need to trust the one in charge of making the best happen. Alas, the analysis becomes circular until we grasp the **holiness** of God.

> If we want to trust that the best is yet to come, we need to trust the one in charge of making the best happen.

Do you know anyone who is holy? Let me rephrase: do you know any human being who has never lied and has always followed through on his or her word?

Neither do I.

No one I know, myself included, has been consistently trustworthy without a single slip-up. Even the Apostle Paul lamented, "For I do not understand my own actions. For I do not do what I want, but I do the very thing I hate" (Rom. 7:15). Despite our best intentions, we fall short. The Apostle Peter, the rock of the church, pledged to never forsake Jesus. "Even if I must die with you, I will not deny you!" (Matt. 26:35). Yet that very night Peter proved his fallibility by exclaiming, "I do not know the man" —not once, not twice, but *three times.*[71]

Today it is not uncommon for the word "holy" to be tossed around in conversation without much thought. The urban dictionary defines "holy" as merely a sentence amplifier or "to exaggerate the feeling of surprise such as "holy cow!" However, the standard dictionary defines "holy" as "set apart for the service of God or of a divine being; sacred."[72] The classic definition differs from the contemporary version for an understandable reason. True holiness is not something humans possess, and thus, it is difficult for humans to comprehend.

In his article entitled "Holiness Beyond Words," David Mathis notes the conundrum. He quotes John Piper who said,

> "[E]very effort to define the holiness of God ultimately winds up by saying: God is holy means God is God.... The very god-ness of God means that he is separate from all that is not God. There is an infinite qualitative difference between Creator and creature. God is one of a kind. Sui generis. In a class by himself. In that sense he is utterly holy. But then you have said no more than that he is God."[73]

The Catch-22 of holiness resides in the fact that because

---

71 See Luke 22:54–62; Matthew 26:69–75.

72 Merriam-Webster, s.v. "Holy," www.merriam-webster.com/dictionary/holy, accessed July 11, 2016.

73 David Mathis, "Holiness Beyond Words" *desiringGod.org*, August 23, 2012, accessed July 11, 2016 http://www.desiringgod.org/articles/holiness-beyond-words.

God is holy, He is separate, distinct, and superior to everything else. Anything inferior, or created, cannot, therefore, fully possess nor even comprehend God's holiness. "'To whom then will you compare me, that I should be like him?' says the Holy One" (Isa. 40:25).

God's perfection defines perfect. His goodness sets the standard for good. His gloriousness delineates glory. His holiness *is* holy. To understand holiness requires an understanding of God. To understand God requires an understanding of holiness. Hence, a Catch-22.

God made humans in His image, and as such humans share many of His characteristics. Holiness, however, is not one of them. The Bible does call people to imitate God's holiness, but such calling has an entirely different dimension when applied to humans than when it emanates from the essence of the God of the universe.[74] We *strive* to be holy by separating ourselves from sin and dedicating our lives to God. We can work toward holiness, but we will never completely set ourselves

> To understand holiness requires an understanding of God. To understand God requires an understanding of holiness.

apart from sin by our own efforts. Because of the fall of humanity through Adam and Eve, none of us can attain righteousness on our own; no matter how hard we may try. Therefore, none of us, even on our best day, can *be* holy.

The character Forrest Gump made famous the line "stupid is as stupid does" in the 1994 blockbuster movie by the same

---

74   See Leviticus 11:44, 20:26; 1 Peter 1:15–16.

name. Forrest was a man of limited intelligence, but on whom fate seemed to smile. His mother taught him not to limit the standard of his life to his intellectual disabilities. Follow the rules and everything will work out. So he did. And everything seemed to work out, until the love of his life died.

Like Forest Gump's measure of success, we measure our worth by what we accomplish by our actions. If we do not act stupid, we must not be stupid. Such a measure amounts to nothing more than an inconsistent standard, for everything is relative, and much is left to chance. In the end, Gump discovered that life will disappoint because people disappoint. Our bodies fail.

The standard of God's character, however, can only be measured against Himself because there is no higher standard. "For when God made the promise to Abraham, since He had no one great by whom he could swear, he swore by Himself" (Heb. 6:13). God is the essence of His actions. For example, God is not "just" because He enacts justice, God enacts justice because He is the essence of "just." In other words, God's actions do not make Him who He is. God's actions *reflect* who He is. God's deeds, therefore, cannot fall short of His perfect, holy character.

In this way, God does not have to strive to be holy. God is the *essence* of holiness. Holiness is the warranty that God applies to all of His promises.

Humans, however, are nice until they aren't. They are generous until they decide not to be. Humans are ambivalent, fallen sinners who cannot materialize anything purely good.

Remember the part of the movie *Wizard of Oz* when

Dorothy and her quirky companions tentatively approach the throne room of the Great Oz in the Emerald City? They needed the "powerful" wizard to transform their lives. His booming voice and supernatural appearance made him the likely choice to get the job done. To their dismay (and perhaps to ours), it turned out that he was merely a little man behind a curtain, disguising his voice and casting invented images on a screen. He held no superior powers, insights, or abilities. He was a sham. Dorothy and her friends were left "holding the bag." In a moment, all hope was gone as they realized they had relied on promises that a mere mortal could not fulfill.

The Wizard of Oz points out the obvious: *who* controls our future matters. If it is merely a mortal behind a curtain, all hope that he can accomplish the best is lost. Oz, The Great and Powerful, was merely a man. Man is not God. The "powerful" but unholy Oz could not back up his word; he was only an empty promiser.

A *Psychology Today* article entitled "The Empty Promiser" had this to say about those who make promises they cannot keep:

> "They say they'll do something and they never do. Even if the other person fulfills some sort of imposed condition on their compliance, they find a way to renege at the last minute. This sort of behavior teaches children that lie that words don't really mean anything, that words can be used to manipulate other people to do what we

want, and that we don't have to live up to our promises."[75]

The article ends, "When we fail to live up to our promises, we teach those around us that we don't value them enough to follow through."[76] Jantz's observation of the empty promiser describes every person. None of us are any better than Oz, the elusive man behind the curtain. We humans are bound to renege, lie, and manipulate despite our best intentions. Rest assured, "God is not man, that he should lie, or a son of man, that he should change his mind. Has he said, and will he not do it? Or has he spoken, and will he not fulfill it?" (Num. 23:19).

If God's holy character did not assure us that He will follow through on His promise that the best is yet to come, we would be no better off than putting our hopes on the inept man behind the curtain. Thank goodness God is a holy God. He will never go back on His word. He always follows through on His promises. His holy warranty requires it.

God's holiness makes Him like no other. It elevates His standard of trustworthiness to the solid, unwavering rock upon which we can entrust our future. "For our heart is glad in him, because we trust in his holy name" (Ps. 33:21). Everything God does and says about the past, present, and future is backed by

75 Gregory L. Jantz Ph.D. "The Empty Promiser: Has someone destroyed your faith in their good word?" Aug 7, 2013, *Psychology Today*, accessed July 11, 2016, www.psychologytoday.com/blog/hope-relationships/201308/the-empty-promiser.

76 Ibid.

His holy warranty, guaranteeing the best for those who put their trust in Him.

In addition, God's holiness means all His rules, standards, and promises will be enforced on everyone equally and consistently. His consistency engenders a sense of security because God's holy standards have our best interests in mind.

For example, King David was a man after God's own heart.[77] He was the youngest and least likely to be exalted. Yet he defeated Goliath, becoming a legend for millenniums (1

> His consistency engenders a sense of security because God's holy standards have our best interests in mind.

Sam. 17). Even though God had predestined David to be the king of Israel and ancestor of the Messiah, he, like all of us, dealt with personal issues. His own father-in-law tried to kill him on several occasions (1 Sam. 19). As mentioned, after he became king, he fell into the temptation of adultery and even had his mistress's husband killed (2 Sam. 11). Yikes.

Just like with any of us, there were consequences for David's poor choices. God took away the love child from his unholy union with Bathsheba. He also didn't allow David to build God's temple. Yet, just like with any of us, God always forgave when David repented. God doesn't play favorites, but He is true to His promises. David carried the covenant promise that the Messiah would come through him. David's repentance paved the way to fulfillment of this purpose.

We carry a promise too—the covenant promise of being a

---

77   See 1 Samuel 13:14.

spiritual heir of another servant of God who was more faithful than perfect: Abraham.[78] We have the promise of coming under the Abrahamic covenant and to eternal life through Jesus Christ. Once someone who is written in the Book of Life truly accepts Jesus, they never have to wonder if they are saved or not.[79] It's a promise, and God keeps His promises, just like a holy contract.

In a proverbial coin toss, holiness always lands "good" side up. "If you then, who are evil, know how to give good gifts to

> In a proverbial coin toss, holiness always lands "good" side up.

your children, how much more will the Heavenly Father give the Holy Spirit to those who ask him!" (Luke 11:13). The gift of the Holy Spirit is better than the good gifts we give to our children. Even when God's holiness requires following through on judgment, such judgment will still result in good. If it leads to our repentance, it is the ultimate good because it restores relationship with our Heavenly Father, opens the door for our purpose, and confirms the promise to experience the best that is to come.

As difficult as it is for us to admit, because God is holy, He does not have to satisfy *our* idea of goodness and equity. We simply must trust that our holy God knows the result of everything He does. And if we don't? God's plan will prevail

---

78 Galatians 3:29 states, "And if you are Christ's, then you are Abraham's offspring, heirs according to promise."

79 "And all who dwell on earth will worship it, everyone whose *name has not been written before the foundation of the world in the book of life* of the Lamb who was slain" (Rev. 13:8, italics added).

regardless. "Declaring the end from the beginning and from ancient times things not yet done, saying, 'My counsel shall stand, and I will accomplish all my purpose'" (Isa. 46:10). We will be humbled by God's holiness. The question is whether we will be humbled the easy way or the hard way.

Thank goodness God is holy. Our future is secure solely because of this holy qualifier. Our hearts give thanks to the Lord in all circumstances when we honor the holiness of God. "Rejoice in the Lord, O you righteous, and give thanks to his holy name!" (Ps. 97:12). Any less of a holy standard for the One in control of creation and history would send this world spinning out of control.

Holiness captures God's omnibenevolence, omniscience, omnipresence, and omnipotence. He operates outside of this world while affecting the most personal matters inside this world. Holiness captures the supernatural power behind the force of God. God's awesome accomplishments point out that God has done great things for you and me that we could never have done for ourselves. Why? "Holy is His name" (Luke 1:49).

When God's holiness is put into action, we get the benefit of His holy grace, justice, and hope. The benefit? The *best* inheritance.

> "And we have a priceless inheritance—an inheritance that is kept in heaven for you, pure and undefiled, beyond the reach of change and decay. And through your faith, God is protecting you by his power until you receive this salvation, which is ready to be revealed on the last day for all to see." (1 Pet. 1:4–5, NLT).

My family has grown fond of the cooking channel. In fact, I probably enjoy watching the culinary episodes more than attempting their culinary lessons. If you were to ask any of my children, they would all agree that cooking is not my strongest skill. I want to eat the delicious dishes; I just can't seem to get my dishes to be delicious. So we watch, and I try to learn.

One technique I thought I might be able to master is the reduction. I watched several chefs take a cup of liquid, bring it to a boil until all but about a quarter of the original liquid had evaporated. What remained was a more concentrated, focused, and intense flavor of the original.

Well, it's not as easy as it looks. Not boiled enough, and the watery mixture makes a mess of the dish. Boiled too much, and it becomes more of a glue that you can't get out of your pan. Somehow, I've been able to "perfect" these extremes, but not the ideal middle.

I may not be able to make a perfect reduction, but God can. As we discussed, holiness qualifies all of God's attributes. I dare to say, if we put holiness into the pot of eschatology and reduce it to its most focused characteristics, I believe we would be left with a concentrated pot of grace, justice, and hope.[80]

True, God has other characteristics that define Him, and

---

80 God has many attributes, and because of holiness, all of them materialize into His promises. God has also made many other promises—too many to count. Every page of the Bible is filled with statements of God's plans, promises, and exhibitions of His character. If I wrote about every one, there would not be enough pages to exhaust the topics. It is outside the scope of this book to review every aspect of God's character and every promise in the Bible. Suffice it to say, as the time for the end of the Age draws near, the goal of this book is to help you grasp the significance

all of God's characteristics can and should be trusted. But God knows we humans will struggle with the questions about future judgment that can be adequately answered if we understand His holy version of grace, justice, and hope. Over and over again in Scripture, God has shown us that the best is yet to come: it is our inheritance that is kept in heaven for us. This inheritance is guaranteed for those who trust in Jesus. In fact, it is being shielded by God's power as we speak.

> But God knows we humans will struggle with the questions about future judgment that can be adequately answered if we understand His holy version of grace, justice, and hope.

Why focus on grace, justice, and hope when there are so many ways to define the incomparable God of the universe? When I set out to write a study on the end times, God asked my spirit, "How would you summarize the Book of Revelation?" I did not hesitate to answer, "I would summarize it as grace, justice, and hope." God gave me a sign through these words that out of all His incomparable characteristics, grace, justice, and hope provide ample guidance to understand His overarching purpose.

The three promises work hand-in-hand beautifully. If the definition of holy grace is getting something we do not deserve, then holy justice can be defined as always getting what we deserve. It follows then, that holy hope is confidence that the holy standard of grace and justice will be applied equally and

---

of His holy version of grace and justice and give you hope to carry you through.

consistently. Because His holiness makes God faithful to His promises, we know His execution of grace and justice will be perfect and complete, giving us hope for the future.

Unfortunately, because of our sins, the only thing we actually deserve is the consequence of sin—spiritual death. Who hopes for that? None of us. Yet don't we hope that criminals get what they deserve? Such is the standard of human justice, which is not very appealing when the table is turned and we are on the receiving end of such justice.

> Because His holiness makes God faithful to His promises, we know His execution of grace and justice will be perfect and complete, giving us hope for the future.

Rest assured, a holy God can only give us what we deserve. And that's good news because through His Son, we deserve life, not death. God gave His Son, Jesus, to serve as our surrogate blood sacrifice, enduring death and resurrection for our sin. The eschatological impact of knowing that the one who gauges what you deserve always executes perfect grace and justice garners pure hope. God cannot get it wrong. And that makes entrusting His promise of the "best" so right. Jesus stands in the place of our punishment, getting what we deserve on our behalf. And we in turn get what He deserves—an eternity in the loving arms of our Creator God.

In light of God's overarching plan of redemption, there are events that have not yet occurred. It is worth reiterating that while victory over sin and death has been secured by Jesus Christ's resurrection, full possession has not yet come to fruition. Just like an inheritance, it is waiting for us, secured by our holy trustee, until the proper time.

Perhaps this causes you to scratch your head. We cannot imagine winning the lottery and instead of a payout, receiving a note stating "Congratulations! You won! Your reward will be available for your full possession at an unknown time in the future." Too much could happen in the interim to sabotage the windfall. What if the economy collapses or someone misplaces the ticket? What if you do not live to spend it? The scenario offers too little security to hold out. So, why does God ask us to wait? The full execution of God's plan must be timed impeccably to include everyone whose name is written in the Book of Life.

Scripture says, "Having cancelled the charge of our legal indebtedness, which stood against us and condemned us; he has taken it away, nailing it to the cross" (Col. 2:14, NIV).

As mentioned, everyone who has faith in Jesus Christ as God's Son who died and was raised from the dead has his or her sin nailed to the cross with Jesus. Jesus's blood sacrifice pays the death penalty for our sin. Be warned, however, that the serpent wants to take with him everything not nailed to the cross with Jesus. "The thief comes only to steal and kill and destroy. I came that they may have life and have it abundantly" (John 10:10).

When the storms of judgment come, believers will be safe on the boat with Jesus. Without Christ, however, our sinful hearts are going to tether us to a sinking ship of judgment and we, along with our sin, will experience the second death.

Thankfully, God's patience means our salvation. God's

patience is being tested everyday that He does not simply drop

Thankfully, God's patience means our salvation. God's patience is being tested everyday that He does not simply drop the curtain on the opportunity for redemption.

the curtain on the opportunity for redemption. God has not yet closed the doors on the chance for spiritual salvation so that more people will accept his offer of grace. Will you?

*Dear God, thank you for your **holy** grace and justice, which gives me hope for the future. I need not fear knowing that you are in control because you are always fair and just. I praise your holy name for giving me what I deserve by giving me something I do not deserve—your Son, Jesus. When I think of the alternative, of not having a benevolent God whose grace surpasses human understanding, I realize we would be in so much trouble. We have you, though, and so we will be better than okay; we will be safe and secure, loved and lifted up to be with you for eternity. To you be the glory. In Jesus's name, Amen.*

CHAPTER

ELEVEN

GRACE: GETTING SOMETHING WE DON'T DESERVE

*"But God shows his love for us in that while
we were still sinners, Christ died for us."*

~Romans 5:8

W hat's the nicest thing anyone has ever done for you? In 1984, Mrs. Hubbard guided a group of twenty-four third graders through reading, writing, and 'rithmetic (and dare I say, "rule following"). Of the subjects, rule following posed the biggest challenge for the eight-year-olds. A growing familiarity with classmates increased the desire to socialize.

In the days before texting and social media, kids wrote notes to each other *on paper*. Even though a rule forbade passing notes in class, often the temptation proved too much.

One afternoon, a note of particular significance made its way through the fingers of several students in Mrs. Hubbard's class before she asked, "What's that?"

The perpetrator (myself) was caught red-handed. I had to accept the consequence—move my desk next to the teacher. If I couldn't be trusted, I would have to be watched. As humiliating as that was, my mind raced with thoughts of what my *dad* would do when he found out. I could not focus the rest of the day. The closer it got to dismissal, the more my angst grew. As the bell rang and I gathered my belongings, Mrs. Hubbard called me over. She leaned over and said, "I won't tell your dad."

How did she know? What a relief. Mrs. Hubbard held to her word. She even gave my parents a glowing report about my "good" behavior. Mrs. Hubbard gave me something I did not deserve. She not only mitigated further punishment from my parents, she gave me a cushion of *grace*.

Humans are hardwired for love. Getting something we don't deserve evidences love. Since "grace" is getting something we don't deserve, it follows that grace is an act of love. We want grace. Yet, when we are offered something without having to prove ourselves or without owing anything in return, we grow suspicious.

Humans are hardwired for love.

Young children learn early whether grace can be trusted. If, for example, fathers relate to children in loving ways and prove their love with their consistent, trustworthy, and disciplined (re) actions, the child might grow to recognize grace as love. Sadly, for many, their childhoods did not include such fatherly "love."

Perhaps your father was "no good." Perhaps you tried in vain to earn the fatherly love you so desired. Perhaps your father was not present in your life at all. You may not even have a father. If you fall into any of these categories, it may be hard for you to understand and trust the love of a Heavenly Father.

One Father's Day, a friend quietly noted that for her, the holiday does not conjure happy feelings and special memories. For her, Father's Day marks a sad time realizing all she never had in a father. Her father showed his "love" through disappointment and reneged promises, no-shows, and general disinterest. Growing up, she wondered what she had done so wrong for her father to reject her. She lamented whether she was the only one for whom Father's Day failed to measure up to the celebratory holiday it was meant to be.

A few years ago, a video went viral of a baby's reaction to his mother singing Chris Tomlin's song "Good Good Father."[81] Happy tears welled in the baby's eyes as his mother serenaded the lyrics to him. This baby, albeit young, innately reacted to the praise for the love of his Heavenly Father. Why? As Tomlin's song recites, we have a good, good father. It's who He is. And we are loved by Him. *It's who we are.*

True love loves because of who we *are* not because of what we *do*. True love cannot be earned. It is given without merit.

---

81 Chris Tomlin, "Good Good Father," from the album *Never Lose Sight*, Sixsteps, October 2, 2015, Songwriters Tony Brown and Pat Barrett, produced by Ed Cash, Jeremy Edwardson, and Ross Copperman.

True love is getting love even though you don't necessarily "deserve" it. Tomlin got it right—we are loved by God. It's who

> True love loves because of who we *are* not because of what we *do*.

we *are*—a people made to be loved by our Creator. Despite the aggravation, our hormonal teen, our tantruming toddler, our stressed spouse all receive our love despite their actions because of who they are to us—family. That's not to say that at times hurtful emotions might push us to the point where the line between love and animosity is blurred. Thankfully, the line for God's love for us is never blurred. We are His children—His family.

That's not to say God does not hate. God righteously hates what separates Him from what He loves—you and me. Sin draws us away from Him and prevents us from reaping the full benefits of His love. Make no mistake, however, He never hates you.

Our Father in heaven loves us this way. "But God shows his love for us in that while we were still sinners, *Christ died for us*." (Rom. 5:8). In the face of the sin that is pulling God's children away from Him, God's love moved Him to do something. Jesus offers His surrogate sacrifice to all of us while we are still committing the crimes for which Jesus was condemned to die. He gave up His life to bridge the gap between our sin and His holiness.

God makes it clear, if we want what He offers, we need not wait until we clean up our act to accept His offer. There are no strings attached; no proving ourselves; and no indebtedness. That's grace.

God could merely give us mercy and cancel the punishment for our sin. But such cancellation would only last until we commit the next crime, which the Lord knows is inevitable given our corrupted flesh, the world, and the devil. Holy God offers something more, something that supersedes even mercy. What God offers we did not earn, cannot earn, and will not earn. He is gifting us something we do not deserve. He is gifting us grace.

> What God offers we did not earn, cannot earn, and will not earn. He is gifting us something we do not deserve. He is gifting us grace.

Our Heavenly Father offers us grace in the form of His own Son, Jesus Christ. God did something so selfless that the measure of His love transcends all human love. God's love rises to a greater, supernatural standard that most mortals would shudder to imitate. That is the essence of God's holy grace—the sacrifice of His own Son for the lives of others while they are in the process of betraying Him.

Jesus Christ *is* the pre-eminent manifestation of God's holy grace. As Max Lucado stated in his book *Grace: More Than We Can Image; Greater Than We Deserve*, "Grace is everything Jesus. Grace lives because he does, works because he works, and matters because Jesus matters."[82] Jesus stands in the place of our punishment, getting what we deserve on our behalf. And we,

---

82   Max Lucado, *Grace: More Than We Deserve, Greater Than We Imagine* (Nashville: Thomas Nelson, 2012), 10.

in turn, get what He deserves—an eternity in the loving arms of Creator God.

It has been said that the value of something can be measured by how much one is willing to give up for it. The value God puts on us equates to the value one would put on the life of His only child. God allowed His Son to be crucified for us. The sacrifice was all God's; the blessing is all ours.

In 1962, Don Richardson and his wife, Carol, moved to West Papua, Indonesia.[83] The couple, along with their six-month-old son, set out as missionaries to disciple a remote and cannibalistic tribe called the Sawi. The faithful family tried hard to earn the trust and respect of their new community with the ultimate aim of sharing the love of Christ. As they slowly learned the primitive language, they came to understand that the Sawi idealized treachery and as such, lacked words into which grace and forgiveness could be translated. Try as they might, the Richardsons were dismayed to realize that the Sawi saw Jesus's betrayer, Judas, as the real hero of the Gospel story. Don needed a way to syncretize the Gospel message to the Sawi people so they could grasp the enormity of God's love and grace for them through Christ's substitute blood sacrifice on their behalf.

Over time, the Sawi grew very fond of the Richardsons. In fact (as no good deed goes unpunished) their benevolence fawned flames of rivalry among sects of the tribe. They soon

---

83 Don Richardson, *Peace Child: An Unforgettable Story of Primitive Jungle Treachery in the 20th Century* (Bloomington, MN: Bethany House Publishers, 2005).

found themselves the cause of savage battles that broke out between various villages.

"Make peace," Don told them, or they would leave. To his surprise, the opposing tribes responded in a most unexpected way. They offered one of their very own newborn babies to the enemy village as a secured promise of peace. As long as the "peace child" remained alive, the warring villages pledged to live in harmony with each other.

The Richardson's were blown away that a father would offer his very own son to ensure peace and reconciliation for an entire generation of Sawi people. Then it hit Don—*this* was the missing link. The peace child became the perfect metaphor for the Gospel. Jesus was the ultimate *peace child*!

Through the metaphor of the peace child, the Sawi accepted Jesus as their Lord and Savior. The Sawi's own sacrificial practice evidenced the immense sacrifice required to ensure peace in a culture that would not trust anything less. What the Sawi could not articulate in words, they articulated in action.

We humans value actions to back up the reliability of others' promises. In our culture, we even have an idiom to capture that sentiment: "actions speak louder than words." We trust the person who is willing to "put up" rather than merely "speak up." Someone willing to give up his or her child in the name of peace is certainly "putting up." The enormous sacrifice of one's own flesh and blood as collateral for someone *else's* bad deed elevates the trustworthiness of that person's word.

We shudder at the very thought of bartering one of our own children to ensure peace with neighbors. The sacrifice certainly gets our attention, and likely incites trust in the person making the promising. The Sawi gave the enemy tribe something they did not deserve: a peace child. God gives us evidence in our own nature and way of operating, even the desires of our heart, that He is giving us something we do not deserve, but it's his pleasure to do so because He loves us.

So I ask, what would it take for you to trust God's promise of grace? What would God have to offer for you to accept His plan through such a free gift leading to eternal life?

While we may not want to accept any less than the Sawi did as collateral for a promise of eternal peace, we realize we don't have to accept less. God was willing to sacrifice His very own Son. Thankfully, the grace God offers is not limited to one generation. The grace of God is not limited to a particular geography or village. The grace God offers is not even limited to this life. We receive the pleasure of God's fulfilled promise of grace both now and for eternity.

> We receive the pleasure of God's fulfilled promise of grace both now and for eternity.

Grace means everything for eternity, but it also has meaning for our everyday lives. When was the last time someone judged you? I bet you remember. I know I do. I also remember feeling the shame from "messing up" and falling to the level of reproach. I remember lamenting to God, wondering why my "judge" hadn't offered *me* grace; maybe a little constructive correction or compassion. As I pored over what I did and what I felt they didn't do, God stopped me dead in my tracks with this, "My grace is sufficient for you, for my power is made perfect in weakness" (2 Cor. 12:9a).

Why do we look for a pass from others when we already received the only pass we need? None of us want to be in a position where our strongholds rear their ugly heads. But when we end up there regardless, we can do what Paul did after he received the clarity about the sufficiency of Christ's grace. Paul decided to boast all the more gladly of his weaknesses, so that the power of Christ may rest upon him! (12:9b).

When we get a taste of Christ's grace, we will sing its praises, "Amazing grace, how sweet the sound that saved a wretch like me. I once was lost but now I'm found, was blind but now I see."[84]

What is it like to have been blind and then see for the first time? The testimony of a man in the first-century has survived to tell us. In the first-century there was no braille system, or mandated accommodations for the disabled, or welfare for those unable to work due to loss of sight. The blind had to rely on family or beg. One such man, having been blind since birth, did just that—begged to survive. Then, one encounter changed everything. The blind man didn't seek out this encounter; the encounter sought him out in order that "the works of God might be displayed in him" (John 9:3).

Imagine sitting by the road waiting for the ting of a coin to fall near your lap when a man calling himself "Jesus" spits in the dirt, makes mud, smears it on your eyes and tells you to go wash it off. You do just that, and as the last of the water falls

---

84 John Newton, *Amazing Grace*, 1779.

from your eyes, light fills where you only knew darkness. You once were blind, but now you see.

For the first time the man saw everything—an overwhelmingly amazing experience. He cried out, "Why, this is an amazing thing!" (John 9:30). When interrogated by his neighbors and the Pharisees, all he could do was recite that he had simply followed Jesus's instructions. The people grew angry that Jesus, a mere mortal in their estimation, performed this miracle without more than some simple spit, dirt, and water.

The reaction to this miracle on the blind man's heart? Belief. The reaction on the heart of the Pharisees and neighbors? Contempt and pride. Jesus said, "If you were blind, you would have no guilt; but now that you say, 'We see,' your guilt remains" (John 9:41).

The blind man tasted God's grace. His eyes had been opened. The light had entered and pierced his heart. The Pharisees did not seek the light. They were wise only in their own "sight." Their pride prevented them from seeing the true light.

All it takes is just one taste of God's grace and our eyes will be opened. Even though Jesus performed this miracle to evidence His glory, we don't need miracles or special revelation to get such a taste of God's grace. Paul taught, "For his invisible attributes, namely, his eternal power and divine nature, have been clearly perceived, ever since the creation of the world, in the things that have been made. So they are without excuse" (Rom. 1:20). God has made His grace available to everyone through creation regardless whether anyone will attribute the miracle of creation to God or not.

Naturalists and secularists claim that this world and even life itself are a result of a random combination of molecules haphazardly connecting in just the right way to produce life and the environment that supports such life. They claim that life spontaneously appeared as a simple multi-cell organism, but has evolved into multiple, more advanced species—all while the subordinate species from which they evolved stay stagnant to continue to subsist in their former state with no further evolution. How do some animals from the same species evolve and others stay the same? This is one of a number of questions about the efficacy of the theory of evolution.

You may believe in *macro*evolution, but there are only theories, no direct proof, of this hypothesis. The complex yet interdependent design of nature—the environment, the cosmos, the various species, the human body, and human conscience—did not randomly appear. While they may evolve on a micro scale within their own kind, there is no evidence that entire kinds of animals morphed into an entirely different kind. Only theories of this happening exist based on microevolution. By the very presence of various, interdependent, and yet wholly distinct kinds in God's creation, we are left "without excuse" as to God's existence.

Don't believe the lie that you are a random occurrence in a meaningless and purposeless existence. You were planned. God chose to make *you* before time began; He knit *you* stitch by stitch in your mother's womb with a unique ability to survive in this made-for-you ecosystem that works in perfect harmony to balance the needs of all life forms. That is grace. God did not have act so personally. What's more? He planned for *you* to spend eternity with Him in heaven. God's sovereign decision to create you did not precede His sovereign decision to save you. "For from his fullness we have all received, grace upon grace" (John 1:16). His grace just does not end.

You know you have gotten a taste of His amazing grace when, after a particular season of travail, you look back with a sense of sadness, mourning the loss of His sweet fellowship uniquely available in those seasons when His grace was ever more crucial. The fellowship is not lost because you are no longer suffering. You fear that the depth and quality of your fellowship with God will fade since your "need" for God's grace has resolved. You wonder if you once again will allow the cares of the world to seep in to replace the companionship you sought with your Heavenly Father during your time of suffering.

> God's sovereign decision to create you did not precede His sovereign decision to save you.

It doesn't have to be this way. "And God is able to make all grace abound to you, so that having all sufficiency in all things at all times, you may abound in every good work" (2 Cor. 9:8). God's grace gives us grace in all things at all times, not just times of difficulty. We use this abundance to share what God's grace through Jesus Christ has done for us. We use this abundance to grow in our capacity to give grace. And we use this abundance to share our gifts of His grace—all to the glory of God.

GRACE & JUDGMENT: TWO SIDES OF THE SAME JUSTICE COIN

*"For the wages of sin is death, but the free gift of
God is eternal life in Christ Jesus our Lord."*

~Romans 6:23

I t never ceases to amaze me the appalling acts one person will perpetrate against another person. We shake our heads at the worst offenders while we secretly harbor hatred in our own hearts. And yet, things are not always as they seem. What appears to be loving might actually be hatred concealed as love. Anyone who has felt the bane of rejection can relate to the deep feeling of love turning into its seething opposite.

When we hear the phrase "two sides of the same coin," usually what comes to mind is the dichotomy of love and hate. One of the greatest examples of this is anytime we associate "hate" with God whom we equate with love.[85] The idea that God could love us so much He would send His Son to suffer and die for our sins, and yet sentence the sinner to eternal death is difficult for us to take. How can we reconcile this apparent contradiction? The answer: The same sin that necessitated His divine sacrifice necessitated a righteous judgment.

What does God's divine sacrifice have in common with God's righteous judgment? They are two sides of the same *justice* coin. God hates, but only for perfect reasons. Usually those reasons are directed at that which separates God from the ones He loves. God's holiness generates a righteous (holy) hatred toward anything that disconnects Him from His children. "But your iniquities have made a separation between you and your God, and your sins have hidden his face from you so that he does not hear" (Isa. 59:2). We can say with certainty that God hates sin. As such, God's righteous hatred of sin forms the basis of God's *just* judgment.

God demonstrates righteous hatred for our sin when He reproves and corrects us, even through very painful circumstances. We do not often understand, but God's plan for His children necessitates sanctification through adversity to purify us for our eternal presence with holy God.

Some of the most righteous people by the world's standards reject God for judging whom they perceive to be well-intentioned people. Perhaps the better question to ask is whether there really are any well-intentioned people? Charles Spurgeon said, "Brother, if any man thinks ill of you, do not be angry with him;

---

85 See Psalm 5:5; 11:5, Malachi 1:2-3.

for you are worse than he thinks you to be."[86] Scripture says, "For all have sinned and fall short of the glory of God" (Rom. 3:23). Thus, while we perceive hate as the antithesis of love, in light of God's holiness they are not mutually exclusive. God's love is equally manifested through His plan to save the sinner and condemn the sin.

Although the two sides of justice seem very different, they are very closely related. Both components of God's righteousness (loves us and hates sin) accomplish the goal of holy justice. The Apostle Paul taught, "For the wages of sin is death, but the free gift of God is eternal life in Christ Jesus our Lord" (Rom. 6:23). This Scripture testifies to the essence of God's holiness carried forth in the duality of God's justice. It explains that while there is a penalty for sin, God provides a way to opt out of that penalty.

Rest assured, the two sides that make up holy justice do not reflect an ambivalent God. God's justice takes two forms because people respond to sin two different ways. We have free will to choose. But our choices have consequences.

If we choose to love sin, we are deliberately choosing to reject our Creator, requiring God to serve the retributive side of His justice coin. If we choose

> God's justice takes two forms because people respond to sin two different ways. We have free will to choose. But our choices have consequences.

to repent of our sin and accept His means of reconciliation,

86   Charles H. Spurgeon, *The Complete Works of Charles H. Spurgeon: Sermons 2001 to 2061*, vol. 34 (Fort Collins, CO: Delmarva Publications, 2013).

God's holy justice requires Him to redeem us from our sin and restore our relationship with Him forever. Both sides execute God's righteousness and, thus, are *just*. God's plan of redemption will end when He serves His final round of holy justice by putting His last enemy under His feet—spiritual death, which is the consequence of our sin.[87]

◈ ONE SIDE: REDEMPTIVE JUSTICE

All people are born into sin, which means we would all fall under God's judgment if not for his holy grace. Redemptive justice (grace) offers believers a "get out of jail free card" (free to us but not to God). When we accept God's gift of grace through Jesus Christ and live accordingly, the consequences of our sin will still be judged, but they will be judged against our substitute sacrifice—Jesus.

The redemptive side of God's justice coin could be summarized as "you do, *I* pay." God's redemptive justice satisfies His holiness by having someone without sin (Jesus) stand in the place of sin's penalty (death), bringing restoration to the true offender. Jesus took the brunt of His own wrath so He could serve us redemptive justice. *That* is love. As Philip Yancy articulated, "Love was compressed for all history in that lonely figure on the cross, who said that he could call down angels at any moment on a rescue mission, but chose not to—because

---

87 This is still to come, although our victory over death has been secured by Christ's death and resurrection.

of us. At Calvary, God accepted his own unbreakable terms of justice."[88]

Those who receive a "get out of jail *free* card" are truly free to live according to the Holy Spirit abiding in their hearts. They are not free, however, to live a life according to their flesh. The freedom given on behalf of Jesus's substitute through Truth is not permissive freedom, it is freedom to live the way we should in order to receive the blessings we really want. It is freedom to repent to fall under the abounding blessings of His redemptive justice. As Merrill confirms, "a proper relationship between God and man is 'the sovereign grace of God and man's response of faith and submissive trust.'"[89] We respond to God's redemptive justice by *freely* submitting to His will for our lives.[90]

◈ THE OTHER SIDE: RETRIBUTIVE JUSTICE

If one side of God's justice offers redemption (through grace), the other side of God's justice offers retribution (through judgment). "God's holy eyes are too pure to look on evil; He cannot tolerate wrongdoing" (Hab. 1:13a, NIV).

God's intolerance for sin requires retribution. If redemptive justice is defined as "you do, I pay," retributive justice would be defined as "you do, *you* pay." God serves retributive justice

---

88 Philip Yancey, quoted by Fritz Chery, "Justice," *biblereasons.com*, July 4, 2020, accessed January 12, 2019, http://biblereasons.com/justice/.

89 Merrill, *The World and the Word*, 508.

90 "And he answered, "You shall love the Lord your God with all your heart and with all your soul and with all your strength and with all your mind, and your neighbor as yourself" (Luke 10:27).

on those who refuse to accept His offer of grace through Jesus Christ. These are the people who "exchanged the truth about God for a lie and worshiped and served the creature rather than the Creator, who is blessed forever! Amen" (Rom. 1:25). In other words, these people love their sin, which reveals the posture of their hearts toward God: hate.

What is the penalty for those who must pay the eternal price for their own sin? God is clear: the payment for sin is death; not only the death of one's physical body, but also, and most importantly, spiritual death of one's soul. Whatever suffering might lead up to one's physical death, you can multiply that by eternity for one's spiritual death.

God's retributive justice plays itself out through the exercise of our free will. According to Romans 1:24 "Therefore God gave them up in the lusts of their hearts to impurity, to the dishonoring of their bodies among themselves." Our mortal hearts veer toward the lie that the world and its idols are sufficient to satisfy our holy hungers. God made us to long for Him. The longing to belong, be known, have purpose, and for comfort and security signal our heart's true desire for our Heavenly Father. "Taste and see that the Lord is good!" (Ps. 34:8). He alone can satisfy these spiritual hungers.

> Our mortal hearts veer toward the lie that the world and its idols are sufficient to satisfy our holy hungers.

We have the choice to look anywhere we want to find fulfillment, peace, and security. More often than not, we will choose to sample the offerings of the world to gratify our spiritual hunger. Please note, if you decide to look for fulfillment, peace, and security anywhere outside of a relationship with your Creator, you are settling for a counterfeit version of truth. Cheap substitutions for God's wisdom will leave you dissatisfied and wanting.[91]

To overcome the feeling of dissatisfaction and emptiness, people will rationalize their decision to act in opposition to God. I'm sure you have heard of people living "their truth." When a popular entertainer was recently asked about his adulterous affairs, he replied, "Why can't I do as I please? It's my life."

What's wrong with that? For one, there is no such thing as subjective truth. By its very definition, "truth" has to be true all the time for all people or else it is not *true*. When we rationalize our choices this way, we are really affirming our brokenness and rejecting our God-given solution. Like this entertainer, we are using our free will as an excuse to make the choice to indulge our flesh and reject God's goodness.

Remember, sin is measured by God's holy standard, not by what your neighbor or this popular entertainer has done. If you believe that you have never rationalized your sin or bowed down to a graven image or lifestyle that caters to your flesh, then you are measuring yourself by the wrong standard. All of us fall short of God's holy standard. And the consequence is spiritual death.

---

91 "Yes, my soul, find rest in God; my hope comes from him. Truly he is my rock and my salvation; he is my fortress, I will not be shaken" (Psalm 62:5-6, NIV).

The important thing in our postmodern world is to jump off the bandwagon of subjective truth so that God and not culture can shape our hearts and minds. If we allow culture to shape our beliefs, we will eventually exalt empty alternatives above God. We will be idolaters.

As surprising as it seems, idolatry is pledging allegiance to any person, lifestyle, or choice that is not God. Idolatry can also be putting our hope in good things such as a spouse, a family member, or even a ministry. Scripture teaches, "If anyone comes to me and does not hate his own father and mother and wife and children and brothers and sisters, yes, and even his own life, he cannot be my disciple" (Luke 14:26). "Hate" might seem like a strong word for our loved ones. God clearly does not want us to hate anyone. But if *anyone*, even a loved one, leads us away from our pure allegiance to God, or requires us to deny Jesus as our Lord and Savior, or steers us away from the truth of Scripture, we are to deny them instead of denying God.

What does this look like when we substitute our need for God's love and approval with familial relationships or a ministry purpose? We may be tempted to conform our ministry to cultural values in order to appeal to a wider audience. We may be tempted to compromise our beliefs for the sake of a child's decision that "works for them" but defies God. We may dilute our convictions to placate a nonbelieving spouse. We may deny Christ in order to stay in the good graces of a wealthy family member. The examples could go on and on. All of these amount to idolatry. The consequence is still spiritual death.

God is clear, we can accept His offer of redemptive justice

and have Jesus serve our death sentence, or we can cling to the lie that everything is good, including our inner voice, and serve our own death sentence. If we choose to love sin and go our own way, we will collide head-on with God's hatred for the same sin. And need we ask who wins?

God's righteous hatred for our rejection does not stem from self-righteousness or ego. God's hatred for anything we worship above Him stems from His holy love and compassion for us. Yahweh demands our complete allegiance because He has preordained the best purpose for our lives. His plan can only be found on the narrow path to eternal life through His redemptive justice.

Bottom line: God's justice will be served one way or the other. We can choose for God's justice to be served on us (retributive) or on God's sacrifice (redemptive). We must ask ourselves: *my* god or *the* God? The holy God of the universe cannot and will not stand idly by as His children veer off course. He will not allow sin to wreak havoc indefinitely. God will follow through on His justice.

JUSTICE: ALWAYS GETTING WHAT WE DESERVE

*"God is just: He will pay back trouble to
those who trouble you and give relief to you
who are troubled, and to us as well."*

~2 Thessalonians 1:6–7, NIV

G od holds Himself to His own legal standards. The
legal definition of "justice" has been defined as "(1)
fairness, (2) moral rightness, (3) a scheme or system
of law in which every person receives [their] due from the
system, including all rights, both natural and legal."[92] Justice
could, therefore, be defined in simpler terms as "always getting
what you deserve."

If we *always* get what we deserve, do we really want justice

---

92 S.v. "justice," *Legal Dictionary,* law.com, accessed December 8, 2017, http://
www.dictionary.law.com/default.aspx?selected=1086.

served? It sounds good when applied to our enemies, but not so much when applied to us. Why? Because we usually judge others based on their worst actions but give ourselves a pass based on our best intentions. Our rationale seems "just" until the tables are turned and our victims are asking for the same justice.

So how exactly does God's holy justice play out in His plan for the end? When we examine the judgment prophesied to occur, we may not like what we read.

> "I looked, and there before me was a pale horse! Its rider was named Death and Hades was following close behind him. They were given power over a fourth of the earth to kill by sword, famine, and plague, and by the wild beasts of the earth" (Rev. 6:8, NIV).

To think that such horrific events stem from a holy God whose actions epitomize perfect and complete justice conflicts with our perception of "just." Regardless of our perspective, even these disturbing scenes exemplify the execution of God's perfect and complete (a.k.a. holy) justice.

God doles out his holy justice for the benefit of believers. God's justice will fall on those who reject him, collaterally benefiting those who receive the brunt of their persecution in this life. The scenes of destruction and death at the end of the Church Age show how God hands out such judgment on those who dig their heels into the ground and lean fully on their own (albeit limited) understanding.

To underscore how this time of future judgment

demonstrates God's justice, it will help to understand how God has executed His justice in the past. The following are two examples where divine justice was served. In each scenario, the perpetrator gets what he or she "deserves." In other words, holy justice served may not play out as we think it should, but nevertheless, God serves it perfectly, completely, and consistently according to His holy will.

◈ SCENARIO NUMBER ONE

There once was a young king, the grandson of arguably the greatest, most powerful earthly ruler of all time. The Bible says, "It is you, O king, who have grown and become strong. Your greatness has grown and reaches to heaven, and your dominion to the ends of the earth" (Dan. 4:22). The kingdom: Babylon in the sixth-century BC. The king: King Belshazzar, son of the evil Merodach, and grandson of the great King Nebuchadnezzar.

Every year Belshazzar held a great feast where the whole night was spent in reveling. The naïve ascendant to the Babylonian throne celebrated by drinking wine with his subjects, eventually deciding to partake in using the gold and silver goblets that his grandfather, Nebuchadnezzar, had taken from the temple in Jerusalem (Dan. 5:2).[93]

At the height of revelry, King Belshazzar led the large group

---

93 Under Nebuchadnezzar's rule, the people of Israel and Judah were taken into captivity in Babylon. The exiles learned the customs and language of Babylon. A few, such as Daniel, received high positions within the Babylonian government for their astute insight and godly wisdom (see Daniel 1:1–7.)

in the idol worship of "gold and silver, bronze, iron, wood and stone. Immediately the fingers of a human hand appeared and wrote on the plaster of the wall. . . . The king's color changed, and his thoughts alarmed him; his limbs gave way, and his knees knocked together" (Dan. 5:4–6). What the hand wrote would reveal how God would serve justice on the young despot and his kingdom—it would be destroyed.

> "And this is the writing that was inscribed: MENE, MENE, TEKEL, and PARSIN. This is the interpretation of the matter: MENE, God has numbered the days of your kingdom and brought it to an end; TEKEL, you have been weighed in the balances and found wanting; PERES, your kingdom is divided and given to the Medes and Persians" (Dan. 5:25–28).

◈ SCENARIO NUMBER TWO

Ancient Assyria. The great city, Nineveh, had emerged as the capital of the Neo-Assyrian Empire on the eastern bank of the Tigris River. Nineveh was drenched in idols of wood, stone, gold, and silver. From the foreigner's perspective, it was a strange sight to behold. To the naturalized citizens therein, the symbols had merely become fixtures in a culture that knew no different. Theologian J. E. Henry, imagines the city through the eyes of a stranger making his way through its streets.

> "On every eminence is a palace, or monument, or idol temple, guarded by symbolic monsters in stone, and adorned in carving of bas-relief with

sacred symbols. The markets fill, the bazaars are alive with multifarious dealing, soldiers and war chariots parade the streets, and the evidences of despotic power and barbaric wealth and heathenish worship, with their inevitable accompaniment of luxury, corruption and violence, abound on every side."[94]

Suddenly a stranger, the prophet Jonah, interrupts their business with a dire warning, "'And he called out, 'Yet forty days, and Nineveh shall be overthrown!'" (Jon. 3:4). For the citizens of Nineveh not familiar with the one true God, Jonah's warning caused much alarm, but they did not know what to do. Thankfully, "the word reached the king of Nineveh, and he arose from his throne, removed his robe, covered himself with sackcloth, and sat in ashes" (6:3). The king then issued a decree for all his people to also "relent and turn from his fierce anger, so that we may not perish" (6:9).

Both of these scenarios represent actual events in history. Both perpetrators likely felt the fear of impending divine retribution. Like all human hearts bent on going their own way, both sovereigns *deserved* retribution.

In the first scenario, King Belshazzar desecrated vessels from the Jewish temple and worshipped idols. In the second scenario, the entire populace of Nineveh was indoctrinated in the practice of idolatry and wickedness. One empire was destroyed and one was saved. The difference in justice may

94 J. E. Henry, "A Heathen City in Sackcloth," *Biblehub.com,* accessed December 8, 2017, http://www.biblehub.com/sermons/auth/henry/a_heathen_city_in_sackcloth.htm.

come as a surprise because perfect justice was executed in both scenarios.

King Belshazzar received retributive justice. The story of King Belshazzar ended with him shaking in his boots. His fear motivated him to seek out the meaning of the words written on the wall, which foretold his imminent death and fall of his kingdom, but he did not repent of his misdeeds. That same night, the Medes, a small country east of Assyria, invaded his palace, defeated the Babylonians, and killed the king. Nearly 200 years before, Isaiah had prophesized that the Medes, who were not yet a separate and independent nation at the time of his prophecy, would be the instrument God would use to destroy Babylon and serve retributive justice on Belshazzar's unrepentant heart.[95]

In the second scenario, the prophet Jonah announced imminent destruction of Nineveh due to the Ninevites' idolatrous practices and beliefs, but they received redemptive justice. Instead of setting themselves up against the Lord of heaven, the people humbled themselves. They immediately "believed God. They called for a fast and put on sackcloth, from the greatest of them to the least of them" (Jon. 3:5). Even the king of Nineveh issued a proclamation asking everyone to cry out to God and turn from his or her evil ways and violence (Jon. 3:6–9). God restored Nineveh despite their long history of heathenism because they acknowledged their sin and turned from it.

---

95 See Isaiah 13:17, "Behold, I am stirring up the Medes against them, who have no regard for silver and do not delight in gold."

Why did one receive redemptive justice and the other retributive justice? The answer: repentance. How can we change the course of our eternities (not to mention our present circumstances) and receive redemptive justice instead of retributive justice? Same way, through repentance.

One heathen kingdom was destroyed, the other was spared. King Belshazzar's kingdom crumbled in inverse proportion of his pride while King of Nineveh's kingdom survived in proportion to the people's humility. The point: God examines the heart to know whether to serve retributive or redemptive justice. "Every way of a man is right in his own eyes, but the Lord weighs the heart" (Prov. 21:2). "I the Lord search the heart and test the mind, to give every man according to his ways, according to the fruits of his deeds" (Jer. 17:10). Only a holy God can accurately and adequately weigh the heart on the heavenly scales of justice.

> Why did one receive redemptive justice and the other retributive justice?

The imagery of a balanced scale is God's goal for justice. Traditional commercial scales have often symbolized justice in both the ancient and modern worlds. Imagine a scale with two equally weighted sides suspended on a center pole. In the ancient world merchants used stones on one side of the scales to balance the agreed-upon price for the items on the other side. The symbol of the scale has survived the millennia as the symbol of balanced and, therefore, fair justice. Unfortunately a system carried out by people does not end up being all that "just."

In the ancient world, merchants often misrepresented the weight of the stones. Sometimes a scale would appear balanced, but an unscrupulous merchant either held his or her finger on the scale or substituted the real stones for imitation ones at the last minute. The unwitting customers walked away short of what they were due. They were literally left holding the empty bag. Around the time of Solomon it is presumed that this form of cheating had become commonplace.[96]

Today, the use of scales in daily commerce has been replaced by other means of ensuring a fair deal. However, the gentrification of technology has not eliminated human injustice. Ecclesiastes 3:16 says, "I saw under the sun that in the place of justice, even there was wickedness, and in the place of righteousness, even there was wickedness." When God measures our hearts on His holy scales of justice, we must balance His holiness. People, however, will never measure up to God's holiness.

The American justice system, for example, requires witnesses to pledge that they will testify truthfully. Yet people still lie under oath. Perjury is a crime punishable by prison and expensive fines. Yet people still perjure themselves. Legally enforceable contracts include penalties for default. Yet people default on contractual obligations.

Since there is no way we can balance God's holiness with our own works, God balanced the scale against our wrongs when Christ atoned for our sins on the cross. Because of Jesus's

---

96 *Ellicott's Commentary for English Readers*, biblehub.com, accessed July 26, 2016, http://biblehub.com/commentaries/proverbs/11-1.htm.

divine nature, His is the only heart that can effectively balance God's holiness. Christ's death and resurrection perfectly offset the numerous sins of mankind weighing down the other side of the scales. God's holy justice requires God to bear His own wrath, for He alone is holy. God's holy justice requires Him to balance His own scales of justice. We just have to accept the substitution.

God graciously satisfies the procedural conditions that give fallible humans all the essential information, power, and presence they inherently lack so no one can argue that God's justice was, well, unjust. Thus, you can never say that God does not love you and want for you to be saved.[97] You can never say you have not had the opportunity to be saved.[98] And you can never say you thought you would have another chance to be saved after you die.[99]

Dear Lord, thank you for loving me and for patiently to waiting for me as I respond to the knock of Christ on my heart. As I read this book, I realize I have been given this and other opportunities to submit my life to You. Please help me because sin is alluring. Help me die to self so that I can live for you. I don't want my life to pass me by while I focus on the pleasures of this world and miss out on a far better eternity. I see my sin for what it is—what separates you and me. I repent and accept you as my Lord and Savior. In Jesus's name, Amen.

---

97   John 3:16; Romans 10:13.

98   John 6:37–40.

99   Hebrews 9:27; John 8:21–24.

HOLY GRACE +
HOLY JUSTICE =
LIVING HOPE

*"Blessed be the God and Father of our Lord Jesus
Christ! According to his great mercy, he has caused
us to be born again to a living hope through the
resurrection of Jesus Christ from the dead."*

~1 Peter 1:3

W hat is "hope?" People offer the sentiment that we "hope" all is well. If circumstances are not too far-gone, we hold out for a "glimmer of hope." If things cannot be turned around, we claim that circumstances are "beyond all hope." The use of "hope" in these varying contexts has one thing in common: the implication that a desirable future event is uncertain and outside of one's control. "Hope," therefore, in the worldly sense points toward a favorable result that is uncertain to occur.

We have all desired for something to happen, only to be disappointed when it does not. We "hoped" to no avail. Take Stephanie's experience, for example. In Stephanie's faded memory, the life she shared with her mom and sister was magical even though they were homeless. She has selective memory of the quality of their life together, but whatever it was, she was certain it was better than the alternative.

She'll never forget the day the life with her mom ended and the alternative began. Her mom drove across state lines and left Stephanie and her sister on an unfamiliar curb. "Go there," her mother pointed, "and give them this envelope." Stephanie took the envelope and watched helplessly as her mother drove away, never to be seen again.

Stephanie spent countless days on that same curb waiting—*hoping* her mother would return. The life she lived in the new house was anything but better. She suffered hardships, rejection, and abuse. The hope that her mother would return kept her spirits up. Sadly, the days of waiting on the curb hoping for her mother to return faded completely.

Stephanie realized the hope she placed in her mother's return had no power to bring her back. Her optimistic expectation offered no certainty and eventually failed. Like Stephanie, our hope becomes just another wish when it is tied to an uncertain future. Like Stephanie, most of us learn at a young age not to put too much hope in people.

Is this the kind of hope we have that God will follow through on His promise that the best is yet to come? Thankfully, no. The hope we have in our Heavenly Father's promise is backed by His holy warranty. All His promises, including that the best is yet to come, are certain to occur.

Should the wait discourage us? Definitely not. God's holiness materializes as the essence of holy hope. God is what He does and does what He is. God's holy hope flows from His holy grace and justice. Thus, our hope in God is perfect, complete, and certain.

The Bible has a special name for "holy" hope. Scripture refers to our optimistic expectation that the best is yet to come as our *living* hope. "Blessed be the God and Father of our Lord Jesus Christ! According to his great mercy, he has caused us to be born again to a *living hope* through the resurrection of Jesus Christ from the dead" (1 Pet. 1:3, emphasis added). The work is finished. The battle is won. Therefore, our hope is based on an inevitable conclusion. Those who receive God's redemptive justice through Jesus can confidently expect God to follow through on His promise for no more tears, no more pain, and no more death.

Such hope founded on God's holiness materializes in a future grounded on so much more than wishful

> Those who receive God's redemptive justice through Jesus can confidently expect God to follow through on His promise for no more tears, no more pain, and no more death.

thinking. It is a living, continual, never-ending, always certain hope secured by the completed work of Jesus Christ. It guarantees the rest of God's plan will unfold as fulfilled promises He made.

Just as Christ rose from the dead, all those who accept

His atonement for their sins will follow suit and rise from the dead to eternal life in the presence of God. "But in fact Christ has been raised from the dead, the firstfruits of those who have fallen asleep" (1 Cor. 15:20). Because Jesus lives eternally, believers will also. To die is not the end of the story for believers. Physical death is just the beginning. It provides a means for us to shed the perishable to receive the imperishable. "I tell you this, brothers: flesh and blood cannot inherit the kingdom of God, nor does the perishable inherit the imperishable" (1 Cor. 15:50).

To believe that the perishable flesh has the final say is to acquit the atrocities of this world without justice. It abdicates responsibility for sin. It offers no place for repentance and, therefore, no path to redemption. It makes this life all there is. And we are left with all the sorrow and pain. Is that the best God has to offer? Where is the hope in that? Paul says it this way:

> "But if there is no resurrection of the dead, then not even Christ has been raised. And if Christ has not been raised, then our preaching is in vain and your faith is in vain. We are even found to be misrepresenting God, because we testified about God that he raised Christ, whom he did not raise if it is true that the dead are not raised. For if the dead are not raised, not even Christ has been raised. And if Christ has not been raised, your faith futile and you are still in your sins. Then those also who have fallen asleep in Christ have perished. If in Christ we have hope

in this life only, we are of all people most to be pitied" (1 Cor. 15:13–19).

Paul teaches us that Christ's death and resurrection provide hope. Although physical death is a reality, His death makes true life, eternal in the heavens with God, possible. C. S. Lewis says it this way: "If I find in myself desires which nothing in this world can satisfy, the only logical explanation is that I was made for another world."[100]

As Scripture notes, "For this world is not our permanent home; we are looking forward to a home yet to come" (Heb. 13:14, NLT). We look forward to this future. Yet this best, albeit promised, is still to come. In the interim, our hope helps us wait.

Therefore, living hope is a gift that keeps on giving. Scripture notes, "But those who wait for the Lord shall renew their strength; they shall mount up with wings like eagles; they will run and not grow weary, they will walk and not faint" (Isa. 40:31). The hope of enduring this life for a better one renews and strengthens our faith until we reach our eternal destination where there are no more tears, pain, or suffering.

Our entire faith is based on this living hope. "Now faith is the assurance of things hoped for, the conviction of things not seen" (Heb. 11:1). There are two key terms here to help characterize the Christian faith: *assurance* and *conviction*. For most people, faith in someone or something has little to do

---

100 C. S. Lewis, *Mere Christianity* (San Francisco: HarperOne, 2015).

with either assurance or conviction. Both are strong words that imply certainty rather than wish.

How can we equate hope with assurance? Only the Christian faith offers an assured hope that things will happen as God promised. Only the Christian faith enables us to be convicted of the truth of things not seen.

The Christian faith can do so because of the *authority* behind the promises. As discussed, our *holy* God is the one who has the requisite power, knowledge, control, and commitment to follow through on the desire, need, and outcome we hope for. Faith based on an assured hope and conviction in what is not seen requires a holy authority behind the faith that is greater than all that is seen in this world. Such authority exists outside this world and He is definitely not limited by this world.

When God told the prophet Jeremiah that he planned to give him a future and a hope, God did not plan to give Jeremiah (or any of us) a genie with a magic lamp to grant him three wishes. The hope God speaks of is assured—it is certain. Jeremiah's circumstances were dire. He was tasked to warn God's people to turn back to God . . . or else. Known as the "weeping prophet," Jeremiah witnessed the destruction of Jerusalem and the Temple and lamented the defeat and exile of His fellow Jews. He was hated, yet he delivered message after message. Jeremiah needed hope that his life of suffering on account of God was not all for naught. God gave it to him (Jer. 29:11). This hope kept him and will keep us afloat in the currents of this life. This hope will keep us heading in the direction God planned for us no matter what obstacles emerge along the way. "May the God of hope fill you with all joy and peace in believing, so that by the power of the Holy Spirit you may abound in hope" (Rom. 15:13). Our hope is based in God's promises of joy and peace that keep us steady and able to endure in the trials between the already and not yet.

Have you heard the story of the man who found himself stranded at sea? He prayed, "Lord save me." So God sent the coastguard. The man replied, "Thank you, but I believe that God will save me." "Suit yourself," the sailor replied and turned the boat around for the shore. "Lord," the man prayed again, "I am trusting that you will save me." So the Lord sent a helicopter. "Grab onto the rope and get into the basket!" the pilot yelled over the roar of the blades. "No, thank you," the man yelled back, "My God is going to save me!" "Suit yourself," said the pilot as he flew away." The man was growing tired, not sure if he could last much longer. "God, please, I beg you to save me," repeated the man in the water. So God sent a raft. The man looked at the raft that could give him rest from his exertion until his savior arrived, but wondered if that evidenced weak faith. So he pushed the raft away. Finally, the man took once last breath before his head sunk below the surface of the water never to be seen again.

In heaven, the man asked God, "Why didn't you save me?" God answered, "I tried! I sent a boat, a helicopter and a raft. You rejected all three!"

Most use this story to illustrate God answering prayer in ways we might not recognize. But I want to showcase the tenacity of the man who endured the adversity at sea. What kept him afloat for so long? His hope in the Lord. His reward? An eternity in heaven. True, he died a physical death, but he did not die a spiritual one. Note: even in this fictional story, God came through for him, despite the fact that he did not recognize God's answers. The point: the certainty of our hope in the Lord can get us through the most difficult circumstances of this life, even physical death, knowing the best is yet to come.

In the end, believers always desire more than this earth or our physical bodies can provide. We hope for what Adam and Eve had in the Garden of Eden before they gave in to temptation. We hope for the permanent binding of the enemy into the pit. We hope for the light with no darkness. Our hope lies in the consummation of all God's promises. And thankfully with our holy God, our hope is more than a wish—it is a certainty.

> Those of us who follow Jesus in faith will enjoy the peace of our present inheritance as we await our best future.

Those of us who follow Jesus in faith will enjoy the peace of our present inheritance as we await our best future. And the certainty of an eternity in God's presence gives us hope to sustain us through whatever circumstances we encounter on earth, including the end of days.

SIGNS OF THE TIMES

"As he sat on the Mount of Olives, the disciples
came to him privately, saying, 'Tell us, when
will these things be, and what will be the sign
of your coming and the end of the age?'"

~**Matthew 24:3**

If you are curious about the Second Coming of Jesus Christ, you're in good company. Even the disciples longed for cues that would signal His return. Throughout history, theologians have pondered over the prophecies outlining the Second Advent of Christ, and for good reason. Jesus's return marks the close of the age of grace, the Church Age, and the culmination of God's holy justice against the sin that separates Him from the objects of His love. Knowledge of what to expect before the close of the age increases our opportunity to prepare and avoid being caught as unrepentant in the crosshairs of God's righteous anger.

The Scripture opening this chapter features the disciples'

question. Did Jesus give them an answer? He did. Jesus gave a lengthy answer that can be found primarily in the twenty-fourth chapter of the Book of Matthew.[101] God wanted to give them and us signs of that future time in order to help us understand the outworking of God's holy justice and enable us to prepare our hearts. The following highlights some of what that time will entail:

1. false christs who deceive,
2. scoffing,
3. wars and rumors of wars,
4. famines and earthquakes in various places,
5. hatred and killing of believers,
6. hatred for one another and falling away from the faith,
7. increased lawlessness,
8. love growing cold, and
9. the Gospel proclaimed throughout the nations of the whole world.

Jesus responded to the disciples' request for information, but the signs He gave might be thought of as, well . . . vague.

Jesus has clearly chosen to keep many of the circumstances surrounding His return a mystery. Even He does not know the exact time God has appointed for Him to judge the world and set up His Millennial kingdom. Why? If God keeps humanity guessing, the ones who care will live as if every day is the last day. If God holds out on the timing, hopefully people in *every*

---

101   Also Mark 13:1–37; Luke 21:5–36.

century and *every* millennium will heed the warning to prepare their hearts for an imminent return of Jesus Christ, and their inevitable meeting at the end of one's life. We must live like the first-century Christians with a zeal for the Lord that reflects hearts anticipating the impending reappearance and judgment of Jesus Christ. If Jesus returns today, will He find you faithful?

If we are looking for a sign of Christ's Second Coming, sadly, false predictions of Christ's return are among them. "For false christs and false prophets will arise and perform great signs and wonders, so as to lead astray, if possible, even the elect" (Matt. 24:24). Scripture exhorts believers to use discernment to weed out these false prophecies from true ones. "Beloved, do not believe every spirit, but test the spirits to see whether they are from God, for many false prophets have gone out into the world" (1 John 4:1).

The Apostle John tells us how to discern: "By this you know the Spirit of God: every spirit that confesses that Jesus Christ has come in the flesh is from God" (1 John 4:2). Those who can profess that Jesus is their Lord and Savior, that He came as a man but yet maintained His divinity, that He atoned for the sin of those who accept His sacrifice and live according to their faith, are sealed by the Holy Spirit until the day of redemption. This we can discern.

Jesus wants us to discern, but He does not want us to

> Jesus wants us to discern, but He does not want us to mock.

mock. In fact, scoffing constitutes another sign of the end of the Church Age. Scripture declares, "Knowing this first of all, that scoffers will come in the last days with scoffing, following their own sinful desires" (2 Pet. 3:3). People throughout time have interpreted the signs as being fulfilled during their lifetimes. We want to interpret obscure future events into the mold of the era in which we live. Even though some signs have been interpreted throughout history as signs that might line up with Matthew 24 and other prophecies, they have not constituted *the* signs Jesus said would precede His Second Coming. Additional puzzle pieces have historically been missing. Despite false alarms, God's plan of redemption continues to move forward. God's plan of reconciliation progresses patiently, not hastily; efficiently, not fruitlessly; and intentionally, not capriciously.

If false alarms have sounded off throughout time, why are scoffers a sign of the end of the age? Answer: mocking dissuades people from believing that a convergence of factors could manifest in the future because they haven't come to fruition in the past. Scoffing differs from discernment. Scoffers mock because they want to deflect divine light away from their sinful choices. "And this is the judgment: the light has come into the world and people loved the darkness rather than light because their works were evil" (John 3:19). In fact, Jesus said that in the end people will double down to follow their own evil desires.

> "For the time is coming when people will not endure sound teaching, but having itching ears they will accumulate for themselves teachers to suit their own passions, and will turn away from listening to the truth and wander off into myths" (2 Tim. 4:3–4).

Mocking allows unrepentant sinners to turn a warning into a perpetration. Mocking allows those on the outside of God's salvation matrix to turn the tables and proverbially "shoot the messenger."

So is it any coincidence that one sign of Christ's glorious reappearing will be an increase in scoffing? When Christ returns to judge everything tethered to that which He righteously hates (sin), those who love sin more than their Heavenly Father will be sadly insulated by a culture that sees right as wrong and wrong as right. In the end, society will view judgment and repentance as extreme and cruel, but infanticide and euthanasia as normal and compassionate.

> "But understand this, that in the last days there will come times of difficulty. For people will be lovers of self, lovers of money, proud, arrogant, abusive, disobedient to parents, ungrateful, unholy, heartless, unappeasable, slanderous, without self-control, brutal, not loving good, treacherous, reckless, swollen with conceit, lovers of pleasure rather than lovers of God, having the appearance of godliness, but denying its power. Avoid such people. For among them are those who creep into households and capture weak women, burdened with sins and led astray by various passions, always learning and never able to arrive at a knowledge of the truth (2 Tim. 3:1–7, KJV).

Have people boasted in ages past? Disobeyed parents? Falsely accused others? Engaged in unnatural sexual relationships? Of course. The state of the human heart has not changed since the fall of Adam and Eve. In the last days of the Church Age, however, few people will identify these acts as "sin." Society will rationalize and accept these behaviors as the norm. The psychology of "group think" and "safety in numbers" will relegate truth tellers to the minority, marginalizing—even invalidating—the truth of the Gospel message.

Jesus Himself warned, "For as were the days of Noah, so will be the coming of the Son of Man" (Matt. 24:37). Much like the return of Jesus, which will happen in the twinkling of an eye, the flood caught humanity off guard and unprepared.[102] The people of Noah's day were warned about the impending deluge, yet the warning fell on deaf ears. So too, as Jesus foretold through parables, in the days preceding the Great Tribulation, the warning signs of Jesus's Second Coming will be ignored.

In the case of Noah, God provided the ark. It took approximately one hundred years to build the ark. No doubt Noah's neighbors gawked at the sight of a huge boat being built on dry land. No doubt Noah's neighbors were invited to repent of their sins and join him on the ark to avoid the devastation to come. Instead, Noah's neighbors scoffed at the warning and went about their business "eating and drinking, marrying and giving in marriage, until the day when Noah entered the ark, and they were unaware until the flood came and swept them all away" (Matt. 24:38–39). If we are not careful, we too will find ourselves "eating and drinking, marrying and giving in marriage" until the Day of the Lord is upon us. If we allow the lures of this life to distract us from preparing our hearts for a

---

102 See 1 Corinthians 15:52.

potentially imminent return of Jesus Christ, we risk missing out on our chance to reconcile with our Creator.

The Lord has made it clear through the covenant with Noah that He will never again destroy all living things on earth with a flood.[103] Alas, there is no chance that a literal ark will appear in the future to warn us of impending doom. We have already been warned.

> If we allow the lures of this life to distract us from preparing our hearts for a potentially imminent return of Jesus Christ, we risk missing out on our chance to reconcile with our Creator.

Now we must watch and prepare. Will we heed the warnings to ready our souls for our last days before the return of Christ? The consequences are too great to miss the boat.

Why don't we understand all the prophecies? It might comfort you to know that not even God's prophets could always unpack the meaning of their own prophecies. Daniel's visions caused him much distress. "I heard, but I did not understand. Then I said, 'O my lord, what shall be the outcome of these things?' He said, 'Go your way, Daniel, for the words are shut up and sealed until the time of the end'" (Dan. 12:8–9).

As part of his divine commission while exiled to Babylon, Daniel interpreted obscure symbols embedded in the emperor's dreams about the future.[104] When it came to Daniel's visions of the end, God did not fill in the gaps of Daniel's understanding.

---

103 See Genesis 8:21–22.

104 See Daniel Chapters 2 and 5. God enabled Daniel to warn King Nebuchadnezzar about the future of his reign over Babylon.

God made His intentions clear: the symbols and visions meant to unpack the time of Christ's Second Coming will not be fully known *until* the time of the end.

However, the Lord did provide Daniel a sign of the end. "Many shall run to and fro, and knowledge shall increase" (Dan. 12:4b). We interpret this to mean travel and information gathering will be made more readily available and accessible. The fact is, knowledge has been increasing ever since the first man and woman were turned out into the fallen world. How can this be interpreted as a sign of Jesus's Second Coming? The sign refers not to the mere increase in knowledge and transportation, but rather to the rate at which these actions will increase toward the end of the Age.

If we analyze the rate of travel and information acquisition today, one can hardly ignore the accelerated pace at which they are expanding. In 2013, *Industry Tap Into News* published an article entitled "Knowledge Doubling Every 12 Months, Soon to be Every 12 Hours." Therein the author noted,

> "Buckminster Fuller created the 'Knowledge Doubling Curve'; he noticed that until 1900 human knowledge doubled approximately every century. By the end of World War II knowledge was doubling every 25 years. . . . According to IBM, the build out of the 'internet of things' will lead to the doubling of knowledge every 12 hours."[105]

---

105 David Russell Schilling, "Knowledge Doubling Every 12 Months, Soon to be Every 12 Hours" *Industry Tap Into News*, April 19, 2013, accessed July 21, 2016,

And that estimation was several years ago. At such an accelerated pace, we can envision a time in the not-so-distant future when knowledge may double every minute, or even every second. We do not know what level of knowledge will usher us into the time of the end, but since the curve of information acquisition is heading drastically upwards, the time is getting closer. Whether or not society has reached the apex of knowledge and transportation required to fulfill Daniel's prophesy signaling the time of the end, we will not know.

Suffice to say, the signs of the end time will come into focus like the details of a distant mountain range. With each step closer, the once-fuzzy details of the terrain will become more precise. Almost suddenly, we may grasp features that we missed from a distance. From afar, we might have speculated about these details, but up close we can clearly discern. With the help of the Holy Spirit and sound study, believers will receive increased clarity the closer time approaches the end. Suddenly, believers may grasp signs that were missed from a distance in previous eras.

Perhaps one of the most significant pieces of the end time puzzle is from the Lesson of the Fig Tree in Matthew 24:32–35.

> "From the fig tree learn its lesson: as soon as its branch becomes tender and puts out its leaves, you know that summer is near. So also, when you see all these things, you know that he is near, at the very gates. Truly, I say to you, this

---

http://www.industrytap.com/knowledge-doubling-every-12-months-soon-to-be-every-12-hours/3950,1.

generation will not pass away until all these things take place. Heaven and earth will pass away, but my words will not pass away."

The fig tree is a New Testament symbol or emblem for Israel. In Joel 1:6–7 God describes a nation that "has come up against my land." This nation has "laid waste to my vine and splintered my *fig tree*." Mark 11:19–26 recounted Jesus's cursing of the fig tree, which thereafter withered. This fig tree had leaves. Jesus might have expected to find fruit on the fig tree (faith), but did not, so He cursed it. There will come a time when faith will be rekindled in Israel. A withered fig tree retains its root. A new tree could bud. At that time, Israel will regain its national privileges. Most biblical scholars agree that the rebirth of national Israel on May 14, 1948 likely satisfies that condition.

The point for us: prepare our hearts spiritually for Jesus's return.

The point for us: prepare our hearts spiritually for Jesus's return. In the Parable of the Ten Virgins, Jesus illustrates what will happen to those whose souls are not ready for His Second Coming.

> "Then the kingdom of heaven will be like ten virgins who took their lamps and went to meet the bridegroom. Five of them were foolish, and five were wise. For when the foolish took their lamps, they took no oil with them, but the wise took flasks of oil with their lamps. As the bridegroom was delayed, they all became drowsy and slept. But at midnight there was a

cry, 'Here is the bridegroom! Come out to meet him.' Then all those virgins rose and trimmed their lamps. And the foolish said to the wise, 'Give us some of your oil, for our lamps are going out.' But the wise answered, saying, 'Since there will not be enough for us and for you, go rather to the dealers and buy for yourselves.' And while they were going to buy, the bridegroom came, and those who were ready went in with him to the marriage feast, and the door was shut. Afterward the other virgins came also, saying, 'Lord, lord, open to us.' But he answered, 'Truly, I say to you, I do not know you.' Watch therefore, for you know neither the day nor the hour" (Matt. 25:1–13).

You may be scratching your head asking, what does that mean?[106] Jesus is using the setting of a wedding feast to help us "see" what will happen when Jesus (the Bridegroom), comes for His bride (the church) at an unexpected hour.

Much like the ten virgins who were present at the door of the wedding feast, the church will be waiting for Christ's Second Coming. Also like the virgins, not everyone in the church will be prepared for His arrival. The oil represents the Holy Spirit.

---

106 Jesus quotes the Prophet Isaiah declaring, "I will open my mouth in parables; I will utter what has been hidden since the foundation of the world" (Matthew 13:35). Parables provide moral lessons using allegory or inanimate objects or people in relationship to one another to compare with life experiences and teach object lessons. They usually employ earthly situations to convey heavenly messages. Jesus uses experiences that would be familiar to His audience so that they will comprehend what He is trying to teach them. Parables can serve to hide the meaning from those who choose to reject God and to give a fuller meaning and understanding to those who believe on the Lord (see Matthew 13:10–15).

Of the virgins in the parable, only five had their lamps full of oil. The five who did not have their lamps full of oil scrambled to find some after the Bridegroom had already arrived. Alas, it was too late. They were shut out of the wedding feast (heaven) forever.

The point is that some people in the church will not be spiritually full of the Holy Spirit at the time of Christ's return. They will be motivated to prepare suddenly when the Bridegroom arrives, only to find out that time has run out. The doors to an eternity in heaven will be closed forever.

Jesus is specifically addressing the church in this parable, but the warning applies to both believers and unbelievers. For the church, although many of us are present in our congregations on Sundays, on Easter, or on Christmas, we are not all spiritually prepared for the arrival of our Bridegroom, Jesus Christ. Jesus is trying to teach us that being *prepared* is a whole lot different than merely being *present*. For unbelievers, the warning is dire as well. Submit to your Creator and acknowledge your need for a Savior before it is too late.

Jesus follows up with another parable to further explain what happens to those who are not spiritually prepared and find themselves on the wrong side of the door to eternity upon His return.

> "The kingdom of heaven may be compared to a man who sowed good seed in his field, but while his men were sleeping, his enemy came and sowed weeds among the wheat and went away. So when the plants came up and bore grain,

then the weeds appeared also. And the servants of the master of the house came and said to him, 'Master, did you not sow good seed in your field? How then does it have weeds?' He said to them, 'An enemy has done this.' So the servants said to him, 'Then do you want us to go and gather them?' But he said, 'No, lest in gathering the weeds you root up the wheat along with them. Let both grow together until the harvest, and at harvest time I will tell the reapers, "Gather the weeds first and bind them in bundles to be burned, but gather the wheat into my barn"''' (Matt. 13:24–30).

In this parable, there are two types of plants: wheat and weeds. These plants represent people of the church, those of true faith and those who feign their faith. The parable paints a sad picture of the church, emphasizing the warning to prepare one's heart for inevitable judgment. God will separate those in the church who truly believe from those with disingenuous faith. Those who feign their faith may look and sound like true believers. They are "religious" people, but they have never repented or accepted Jesus as their Lord

> True salvation can only come through a personal relationship with Jesus, not through rituals, rote prayers, or human intercession.

and Savior. Although religiously devout, they lack a saving relationship with Jesus Christ that manifests in good fruit. And sadly, religion does not matter in God's salvation equation.[107]

---

107 People such as the Pharisees, who assumed they were numbered among the people of God because they obeyed the law (at least in front of anyone

True salvation can only come through a personal relationship with Jesus, not through rituals, rote prayers, or human intercession.[108] While membership in a church, synagogue, or non-profit organization may have its benefits, the list of perks does not include eternal life.

Thankfully, as the parable describes, God will wait until the end to separate unbelievers from the true believers, giving even the "weeds" every chance to come to repentance.[109] Do not mistake God's patience for indifference. As the Apostle Paul urges, "Behold, *now* is the favorable time; behold, *now* is the day of salvation" (2 Cor. 6:2b, emphasis added). Do not delay; repent today. It would behoove all of us not to wait another day distracted by this life to prepare our souls for eternity.

---

watching), closely represent the weeds in the parable. In their hearts they were threatened by the truth spoken of by Jesus. These teachers of the Law did not understand that hating the truth spoken by Jesus identified them with Satan rather than God. They rejected God's truth about their sin and exposed their corrupt hearts. Even when these religious experts professed to be His people and practiced deeds that appeared to be God's work, because of their corrupt motives, their actions were in vain.

108 Jesus said to him, "I am the way, and the truth, and the life. No one comes to the Father except through me" (John 14:6).

109 See 2 Peter 3:9 "The Lord is not slow to fulfill his promise as some count slowness, but is patient toward you, not wishing that any should perish, but that all should reach repentance."

GOD WANTS THE BEST FOR YOU

"In this is love, not that we have loved
God but that he loved us and sent his Son
to be the propitiation for our sins."

~1 John 4:10

We've talked a lot about God's overarching plan for humanity. Yet, our lifespans may come to an end before His design fully materializes. To focus on the Tribulation Period at the end of the age may seem like an exercise in futility considering the personal tribulation you may be dealing with right now. You may question the relevancy of a future time of unequaled distress when the immediate crisis you're tackling is unequaled by your own experience.

Perhaps the notion of a sovereign, holy God reaching into history to redeem His creation seems palatable on a macro level. Have you ever asked, "What about *me*?" The enemy is quick to have you dismiss any notion of a personal God who cares about the minutiae of your life. If you have ever thought, "The Creator of the universe is not going to give a second thought about my life and my inconsequential issues," you are not alone.

> The enemy is quick to have you dismiss any notion of a personal God who cares about the minutiae of your life.

Here's the amazing truth about our holy God. Even if you were the only living soul on earth, Jesus would have died to save you from spiritual death. Luke Chapter 15 provides a parable through which Jesus drives home this point.

> "So he told them this parable: 'What man of you, having a hundred sheep, if he has lost one of them, does not leave the ninety-nine in the open country, and go after the one that is lost, until he finds it? And when he has found it, he lays it on his shoulders, rejoicing. And when he comes home, he calls together his friends and his neighbors, saying to them, "Rejoice with me, for I have found my sheep that was lost." Just so, I tell you, there will be more joy in heaven over one sinner who repents than over ninety-nine righteous persons who need no repentance'" (Luke 15:3–7).

If there is just one fact I pray you walk away knowing, it is that God loves *you*. God wants *you* to have a relationship with Him forever. God desires to commune with *you* for eternity. His entire plan to redeem mankind is focused on *you*.

For many, however, the question of life's meaning boils

down to God versus science: which one is the ultimate truth? For some, it makes more sense to trust in science despite its esoteric claims about man's purpose. One scientist stated, "Man knows at last that he is alone in the universe's unfeeling immensity, out of which he emerged only by chance. His destiny is nowhere spelled out, nor is his duty."[110] This theory relegates life to nothing more than a succession of flukes, undermining a person's ability to authentically and autonomously reason. "Science can often explain what is happening, and it can sometimes forecast the future and distinguish wisdom from folly. But it provides no basis for ethical choice, nor the will to act."[111] Science is not bad. God created science. But science as an end unto itself provides no hope for humanity. We are left with no greater purpose than our random responses to the coincidences of life.

Thankfully, nothing is left up to chance with God. He made each of us for a specific purpose. God gave us the ability to reason so we can respond to His offer of grace. There is no isolation with God because we are not alone in the universe. God is present and He desires a personal relationship with each of His children, individually, including *you.*

Is it hard to accept that kind of love? Is it easier to focus on the pain and suffering of this life under the sun? Remember what happened when Lot's wife looked back at the destruction of Sodom and Gomorrah from which she had just been rescued.

---

110 Jacques Monod, *Chance and Necessity* (Paris: Editions du Seuil, 1971), 180.

111 Franklin M. Harold, *The Way of the Cell: Molecules, Organisms and the Order of Life* (Oxford: Oxford University Press, 2001), 258.

Scripture says God didn't waste a moment transforming her into a pillar of salt (Gen. 19:26). A pillar of salt has no living function. It can bear no pain, feel no joy, and experience none of God's grace. What's the use of being saved from destruction if you keep looking back at the ordeal rather than the redemption in front of you?

> What's the use of being saved from destruction if you keep looking back at the ordeal rather than the redemption in front of you?

Jesus redeemed us from such eternal destruction. Acceptance of His grace through faith gives us hope to endure present suffering. Such hope buoys us through the challenges of this life until we receive full possession of His promised rest.

> "Come to me, all who labor and are heavy laden, and I will give you rest. Take my yoke upon you, and learn from me, for I am gentle and lowly in heart, and you will find rest for your souls. For my yoke is easy, and my burden is light" (Matt. 11:28–30).

Can you accept Christ's yoke that promises to be lighter than the one you're dragging around right now?

Race car drivers understand the lesson of focus-based destination.

> "In racing, they say that your car goes where your eyes go. The driver who cannot tear his eyes away from the wall as he spins out of control will meet that wall; the driver who looks down

the track as he feels his tires break free will regain control of his vehicle."[112]

Similarly, where we set our spiritual eyes determines our eternal destination. Our hearts are our steering wheel. The Bible says, "For as he thinketh in his heart, so is he" (Prov. 23:7, KJV). When we believe in Jesus as our Lord and Savior, living in faith, we become the righteousness of God. If we focus on who we are and what we have in Christ, we will reap the blessings of staying on the narrow road to life. If we instead focus on the distractions of the world or a preoccupation with our past, we will crash and burn.

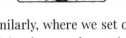

> Similarly, where we set our spiritual eyes determines our eternal destination. Our hearts are our steering wheel.

Depending on the track, drivers start their race without a view of the finish line. Yet, they know it is there. Their focus is on the road that leads to their destination. If they lose focus they are apt never to make it. So too, we do not have a physical view of our eternal finish line. But, we know it is there. Our present focus has to be on the living hope we have in Jesus who leads us to our final destination. "For in this hope we were saved. Now hope that is seen is not hope. For who hopes for what he sees? But if we hope for what we do not see, we wait for it with patience" (Rom. 8:24–25). We patiently stay the course that gets us to the prize of eternal life for which we are racing.

---

112 Garth Stein, *The Art of Racing in the Rain: A Novel* (New York: Harper, 2008).

If we do lose focus, we can rest assured that God's love will never leave us. His mercies are new every morning. His love never ceases (Lam. 3:22–23). No matter what choice you make today, you have the ability to turn from that choice tomorrow, no looking back.

I sometimes read a book to my kids before bedtime. I choose carefully one that will span the ages of my oldest three children. A book that caught their attention was *The Boy Who Harnessed the Wind*, by William Kamkwamba.[113] Kamkwamba grew up in a tiny village in Malawi, Africa. Plagued by poverty and living at the whim of the elements, he and his family nearly died from famine that swept the area after a drought in 2001. A curious boy, Kamkwamba dissected every electronic object that he could find. Finally fed up with the devastating conditions, he took the initiative to build a windmill to produce electricity, something unheard of in his community. Mocked by his peers, Kamkwamba's tenacity and ingenuity paid off when one day he lit a light bulb from the energy produced from his makeshift windmill. In that moment, his creation took form and seemingly gave life to a poverty-stricken village.

Creating the windmill, however, turned out to be only one hurdle. Kamkwamba quickly encountered the challenge of its maintenance. The handmade windmill often broke, requiring hours of painstaking labor to repair. Kamkwamba lamented:

> "Looking up, I saw the chain dancing loose over the crankset while the blades spun wild. When

---

113 William Kamkwamba, *The Boy Who Harnessed the Wind* (New York: Puffin Books, 2015).

I reached the top, I wrapped my legs around the rungs for support. But in trying to keep my balance, I didn't see the bicycle frame swing toward me. Before I could react, the wind sent the blades straight into my hand. The impact knocked me off my feet, and I barely managed to hold on. Looking down, all I saw was blood. Three of my knuckles were now missing their skin. *"'You are my creation!' I shouted to my windmill. 'So why are you trying to destroy me? Please, let me help you.'"*[114]

As I read, I imagined God, our Creator, crying out to us in much the same manner. The windmill seemed to reject the assistance of the only person able to help it—its creator, Kamkwamba. No one else knew how it was assembled and how to repair the damage.

Like the broken crankset on the windmill, we too are broken. And like Kamkwamba's bloody knuckles, our brokenness hurts God. All of this hurt stems from our sin. Our sin separates us from our Creator who is trying to help us. If we don't acknowledge what our sin has done, is doing, and will continue to do, we will never realize our need for a Savior.

Like Kamkwamba, God is crying out to us to accept His offer of help. Only God knows how we are made and what it will take to fix us in our sin. And God's solution? His Son, Jesus Christ. Jesus reattaches our broken chain to God. Only through the blood of Christ can we be reunited and functioning properly.

---

114 Ibid., 222.

When we resist God's help, we allow our sin to destroy our relationship with God.

True freedom to enjoy life to the fullest, to experience the best this life has to offer, only exists under the authority of God.

True freedom to enjoy life to the fullest, to experience the best this life has to offer, only exists under the authority of God. Satan wants to deceive us into thinking God's boundaries limit the pleasures of this life. Satan will appeal to our pride just as he appealed to Eve's pride. We must be aware of the schemes of the enemy so we can recognize them and resist. The safest place to be is within the will of God.

For those who choose to remain outside the will of God, a restless turmoil will accompany life. Blaise Pascal said it this way:

> "What else does this craving, and this helplessness, proclaim but that there was once in man a true happiness, of which all that now remains is the empty print and trace? This he tries in vain to fill with everything around him, seeking in things that are not there the help he cannot find in those that are, though none can help, since this infinite abyss can be filled only with an infinite and immutable object; in other words by God himself."[115]

God penned your life before you were born. He has a plan for you. And it is good. In the course of seeking His plan, you

---

115 Blaise Pascal, *Pensees* (New York: Penguin Books, 1966), 75.

will find Him. The real spiritual breakthrough happens on the journey. It's a continual giving back of our lives in trust to God. In the process, there will be trials. The purpose of these trials is to strengthen your faith and to pay your testimony

> The purpose of these trials is to strengthen your faith and to pay your testimony forward by telling someone else: I know Him. He's real. He saves. He heals. He transforms.

forward by telling someone else: I know Him. He's real. He saves. He heals. He transforms. Amen.

HEAVEN AWAITS

"Rejoice and be glad, for your reward is great in heaven."

~Matthew 5:12a

I n 1999, Mary took her husband, Bill, on the birthday trip of a lifetime to kayak the beautiful rivers of Chile in South America.[116] As an adventurous couple, Mary and Bill decided to try a less journeyed section of a Chilean river. Little did they know this birthday gift would give back in ways Mary could never have imagined or hoped.

On that fateful trip, Mary's kayak became pinned at the bottom of a waterfall, completely submerging the kayak. Rescue efforts ensued, but the force of the powerful torrents proved too strong to unpin her body.

---

116 Mary C. Neal, *To Heaven and Back: A Doctor's Extraordinary Account of Death, Heaven, Angels, and Life Again: A True Story* (Colorado Springs: WaterBrook Press, 2012).

Here's how she described the moment before death:

> "What happened next surprised even me. Time slowed and, despite knowledge of my predicament and the wild turbulence of the water above me, I felt relaxed, calm, and strangely hopeful. In that moment, I prayed words that seemed to come from outside myself. 'God, your will be done. Not mine, but yours.' I'll never know for sure, but in my heart I believe that's when my journey to heaven and back actually began.[117]

Mary did not merely cease to exist. Instead, as water filled her lungs she "saw the indescribable beauty of heaven, experienced Christ's overwhelming compassion, encountered angels, and was immersed in God's pure love."[118]

Mary is not the only one who has died and gone to heaven only to come back to share their experience. Almost everyone who has had a near death experience (NDE) attests that something extraordinary lies beyond the veil of this life. We might want to deny it now, but the reality will confront us sooner or later.

For the skeptics, the preferred explanation for these NDEs might be the rapid firing of neurons as one passes from life to death. Skeptics prefer to believe that the family members, friends, compassion, love, and angels, etc. are nothing but a mirage from wishful thinking as one's body gives up its last

---

117 Mary C. Neal, 7 Lessons from Heaven (New York: Convergent Books, 2017), 2.
118 Ibid.

breath and a brain depleted of oxygen powers off for the last time.

But ask Mary, or anyone who has experienced the reality of what lies beyond the veil, and they will tell you as Mary does, "No one," she said, "is more astonished by my words than I am. . . . There are simply no earthly words to describe heavenly wonders."[119] When God tells us, "What no eye has seen, nor ear heard, nor the heart of man imagined, what God has prepared for those who love him," He means it (1 Cor. 2:9).

Still, far too many people will allow life to pass them by without claiming the heavenly inheritance that Jesus has reserved for those who put their faith in Him. The consequences of such failure are far too dire, because the lament of our procrastination will last for eternity.

Jesus tells the story of one man who encountered that regret. A rich man chose not to show compassion to a poor beggar who lay at his gate every day. Eventually, they both died. The poor man ascended to Abraham's side in paradise and the rich man descended to Hades in torment. "And he called out, 'Father Abraham, have mercy on me, and send Lazarus to dip the end of his finger in water and cool my tongue, for I am in anguish in this flame'" (Luke 16:24).

In their lifetime Lazarus had asked for similar relief from the rich man—to alleviate his physical suffering. During their lifetime, this request could have easily been answered. Now the tables were turned and the rich man was asking for relief from Lazarus, but the request was not so easily answered. The rich

---

119 Ibid., 2–3.

man was in spiritual anguish. The request for spiritual relief was not within Lazarus's authority. In fact, it was too late. Abraham answered that "a great chasm has been fixed, in order that those who could pass from here to you may not be able, and none may cross from there to us" (Luke 16:26).

As Abraham's response pointed out, once you die, it is too late to prepare spiritually and obtain eternal sustenance and comfort. After death, no one is able to pass over the chasm that separates eternal life from eternal death. Friends, now is the time for salvation.

> Once you die, it is too late to prepare spiritually and obtain eternal sustenance and comfort. After death, no one is able to pass over the chasm that separates eternal life from eternal death.

Jesus currently offers himself as the bridge over this chasm, but that opportunity will not be available indefinitely. Why exchange eternal comfort for eternal torment when you can make the decision today to repent and accept the gift of eternal life through Jesus Christ?

God has redeemed you for an eternity with Him in heaven. So what is heaven like?

◇ HEAVEN IS A FOREVER PARADISE

We have many versions of paradise on earth. Whatever your idea of paradise, what's the one thing that would make it even better? If it lasted forever? It wouldn't be paradise if we knew it ended. "Forever" seems to be the measure of true utopia—satisfying our heart's true desire without end.

Why? People don't really want to love at all times. Even Jesus did not entrust Himself to people because, as Scripture teaches, "He knew all people." He knows what is in human hearts (John 2:24–25). Betrayal, hatred, lust, jealousy, selfishness, and lies. There just is no "forever" in another person. People cannot be trusted.

Yet, we intuitively compare the happiest moments here with the promises of heaven. We have a sense of God in us having been made in His image. "Paradise" seems to be the closest term to align with our expectations. "Truly, I say to you, today you will be with me in Paradise" (Luke 23:43). Jesus comforted the dying criminal on the cross next to Him by telling him his repentance will lead to paradise. As our comfort, our peace, our surrogate, our sustenance, our way, our truth, and our life, *Jesus* is what makes eternity in heaven "paradise."

> As our comfort, our peace, our surrogate, our sustenance, our way, our truth, and our life, *Jesus* is what makes eternity in heaven "paradise."

John Burke wrote extensively about near death experiences (NDE) in his book *Imagine Heaven: Near-Death Experiences, God's Promises, and the Exhilarating Future that Awaits You.*[120] What he discovered from his research is that love is a tie that binds most NDEs

---

120 John Burke, *Imagine Heaven: Near-Death Experiences, God's Promises, and the Exhilarating Future that Awaits You* (Grand Rapids: Baker Books, 2015).

together. But not just any love—a love so strong and pure they never want to leave its presence.

He recites the testimony of one woman, "When I saw that bright light, I felt that someone loved me very much (but no idea who that was). I was very overwhelmed with that bright light. And while I was there I felt the love, and that love I had never felt before."[121]

Another man felt "An astonishing love. A love beyond my wildest imagining. This love knew every unlovable thing about me—the quarrels with my stepmother, my explosive temper, the sex thoughts I could never control, every mean, selfish thought and action since the day I was born—and accepted and loved me just the same."[122]

◈ **HEAVEN HAS MANY MANSIONS**

Why are we enamored with big houses? When I found myself a stay-at-home mom with a new baby, I would give myself a break by buckling her into the car seat to drive around town gawking at the large houses that dotted the Connecticut coastline of Long Island Sound. For long weekends my little family would travel to Newport, Rhode Island, to tour the mansions constructed by the industry moguls of the late nineteenth-century. The Breakers, a summer home of the Vanderbilt family, boasts of five floors with over 125,000 square

---

121 Ibid., 29.

122 Ibid., 23.

feet and 70 rooms. Our humble house could have fit in the foyer with room to spare. We couldn't get enough of the opulence.

Perhaps that desire comes from the true reality in heaven where Jesus doesn't skimp on our abode either. In fact, Jesus is preparing some of the living spaces especially for you and me to call home. "In my Father's house are many mansions: if it were not so, I would have told you. I go to prepare a place for you" (John 14:2, KJV). If home is where the heart is, our home is with Jesus. How sweet that He prepares a palace for you where He is, making you feel right at home.

You may be clinging to your family, your friends, your memories, or your amazing house and think, "It can't get any better. I don't want to give this up." Let me assure you, heaven is a real place where you will live in a real space—and it won't be a college dorm room or even the Vanderbilt Breaker mansion, but it will be so much better. It will be with Jesus.

◈ Heaven Is a City

"For here we have no lasting city, but we seek the city that is to come" (Heb. 13:14). Last year we moved our family back to our middle America roots and settled in a city with a river that flows through it. A greenbelt lines the shores while shining glass windows from the downtown office buildings reflect in its waters below. It can be a pretty awesome sight. When I read about heaven's "downtown," however, I realized our life on earth dimly replicates heaven's glorious attributes.

> "Then the angel showed me the river of the water of life, bright as crystal, flowing from the throne of God and of the Lamb through the middle of the street of the city; also, on either side of the river, the tree of life with its twelve kinds of fruit, yielding its fruit each month. The leaves of the tree were for the healing of the nations" (Rev. 22:1–2).

Heaven, it turns out, is a literal city made by God especially for His children. It includes streets of gold, a tree of life that bears fruit each month, and a river wherein the water of life flows. As opposed to our earthly abode for which we toil, everything in heaven emanates from our spiritual life source. The river is not elemental water that satisfies until we thirst again. Water of life quenches our spiritual thirst indefinitely.

The only thing this city does not have is a sun or a moon. In heaven, if you can imagine, there is no sun or moon to light the day and night because there is no need. Just like the living water and the tree of life satisfy our thirst and hunger, true light permeates heaven from God's satisfying glory.

> "And I saw no temple in the city, for its temple is the Lord God the Almighty and the Lamb. And the city has no need of sun or moon to shine on it, for the glory of God gives it light, and its lamp is the Lamb. By its light will the nations walk, and the kings of the earth will bring their glory into it, and its gates will never be shut by day—and there will be no night there. They will bring into it the glory and the honor of the nations. (Rev. 21:22–26).

God is the true light, which came into the world through Jesus Christ (John 1:9). In heaven the true light will be radiating brighter than the sun without any threat of burn, enabling us to bask in the light of His glory forever.

◈ THERE IS NOTHING EVIL IN HEAVEN

Evil is what makes this life so hard. No one is immune or innocent. We each contribute to the depravity of our world every time we act on our sinful desires. We need not be surprised when others act according to their self-interest at the expense of others, but nevertheless, bad acts still violate our conscience.

> God is the true light, which came into the world through Jesus Christ

Because we have been imbued with a sense of God's holiness, we are offended by unholiness; unless it's our unholiness, because then we usually want a pass. "No longer will there be anything accursed, but the throne of God and of the Lamb will be in it, and his servants will worship him. They will see his face, and his name will be on their foreheads" (Rev. 22:3–4).

In heaven we need not worry about any hypocrisy. Nothing accursed will be present to draw it out of us. In fact, we don't even have it in us anymore. Finally, the sin that was tempted out by the serpent is cleansed completely once and for all. In heaven we will have Christ's name, we will be known by His works, and we will be cleansed by His blood.

◈ HEAVEN HAS TREASURES
THAT NEVER DECAY

Just like big houses, we love beautiful jewels and precious metals. We use these valuable materials to demonstrate our love for others. "Diamonds are forever" from the De Beers campaign evidences our desire for a forever love. If a diamond lasts forever, then giving one evidences your desire for that love to last forever. Perhaps our desire stems from the true reality of heaven, where love really is forever, and where precious jewels and metals are the foundation of all building materials.

> "The wall was built of jasper, while the city was pure gold, like clear glass. The foundations of the wall of the city were adorned with every kind of jewel. The first was jasper, the second sapphire, the third agate, the fourth emerald, the fifth onyx, the sixth carnelian, the seventh chrysolite, the eighth beryl, the ninth topaz, the tenth chrysoprase, the eleventh jacinth, the twelfth amethyst. And the twelve gates were twelve pearls, each of the gates made of a single pearl, and the street of the city was pure gold, like transparent glass" (Rev. 21:18–21).

We drape jewelry and gold, silver, platinum and the like around our necks and on our fingers, even in place of teeth, as a sign of power and authority. These materials don't come cheap. All of heaven will sparkle as the light of love from our Heavenly Father and Lamb of God reflects off the jewels that envelop every aspect of heaven. Our desire for them here on earth points to the other world for which we were created, our heavenly home.

◇ IN HEAVEN WE WILL HAVE GLORIFIED BODIES

When Jesus rose from the dead, He did not directly ascend into heaven. He walked the earth and showed himself to the disciples, among many other people. Jesus had a glorified human body, the first after which every mortal would follow. "The Lord Jesus Christ, who will transform our lowly body to be like his glorious body, by the power that enables him even to subject all things to himself" (Phil. 3:20b-21).

What was Jesus's glorified body like? When Thomas doubted that Jesus had risen from the dead, Jesus appeared to Him. He still had flesh, but it was different—glorified. He still had the holes in which the Roman soldiers had drilled the nails, but they were different—glorified. He could still eat food, but the process was glorified. He could still be present, but the process included appearing seemingly from out of nowhere, transcending time and space—glorified. Glorified bodies are perfect and experience no pain or sorrow.

> In heaven, we will be made completely whole and healed.

We too will have such bodies. There will be no need for identifying marks on our bodies, such as Jesus's scars. In heaven, we will be made completely whole and healed.

◈ IN HEAVEN ALL THINGS ARE NEW

I have five children. That means hand-me-downs are a part of our life. I just love pulling out an old bin of clothes and passing them off as "new" to my five- and three-year-olds. So far, it has worked. But if they're anything like my older children, it won't always be that way. We like new. New cars, new clothes, new furniture—you name it. New is clean, fresh, unspoiled, crisp, special, and only used by

> Friends, death is not the end of our existence. It is only the beginning.

us. In heaven, guess what—the Lord satisfies our heart's desire for new. ALL things will be made new in heaven. "And He who was seated on the throne said, 'Behold, I am making all things new'" (Rev. 21:5).

Nothing will cross over from the old heavens and earth to the new. The new heaven and earth become the eternal abode for those who accepted Jesus as their Lord and Savior and stayed faithful in the face of adversity. The new heaven and earth will always stay "new." God will be there cleansing it with His light and love. Nothing unclean has access to heaven. All has been shut out and separated by an impassable chasm.

> "Then I saw a new heaven and a new earth, for the first heaven and the first earth had passed away, and the sea was no more. And I saw the holy city, new Jerusalem, coming down out of heaven from God, prepared as a bride adorned for her husband. And I heard a loud voice from the throne saying, "Behold, the dwelling place of

God is with man. He will dwell with them, and they will be his people, and God himself will be with them as their God. He will wipe away every tear from their eyes, and death shall be no more, neither shall there be mourning, nor crying, nor pain anymore, for the former things have passed away" (Rev. 21:1–5).

Friends, death is not the end of our existence. It is only the beginning. The longest life on earth is just one trillionth of a second of eternity, and even that estimation is a trillion times too long compared to eternity.

If you knew that a simple decision you make in your lifetime could infinitely change the quality of your everlasting eternity, wouldn't you make it?

Don't let hindsight catch up to you. After you die and get the perspective of the eternity you wish you had, it will be too late. It's time to make the decision that will infinitely change the quality of your eternity. Heaven awaits.

BATTLE PLAN

"For we do not wrestle against flesh and blood, but
against the rulers, against the authorities, against
the cosmic powers over this present darkness, against
the spiritual forces of evil in the heavenly places."

~Ephesians 6:12

I've found that many people measure their uncertain lives by the extent the floor has fallen out from under them. Either the floor has already dropped, there is a foreboding that it is about to drop, or you're standing on solid ground. If you are in the third camp, you may be thinking you're doing okay. The coronavirus hasn't affected your family, you haven't lost your job, and your kids are on a steady course. For you, the world is at least tolerable. But many others are facing a broken life with pieces falling like dominos.

A year ago, Heather and her family moved to their forever home in a new state for a promising opportunity with her husband's company. Within months, the company tightened its financial belt and closed the branch. The change did not worry them. Her husband received a severance package, and with his experience, opportunities would be plentiful. Then in March 2020, everything changed. Her husband was an expert in an industry shut down by Covid. His severance ended. They now had to rely on savings to survive. The floor has not completely fallen out from underneath them, but there's a looming fear that it could.

Do you find yourself in a similar predicament? Most of the world is skating on thin ice. The natural response is stress. Stress is heightened in proportion to fear. Fear makes us do things we might not normally do. And no one wants us to veer from the path of "tried and true" more than the enemy.

So, it should be little surprise that scenarios of increased stress seem to follow times of spiritual renewal and refreshment, times you turned back to God and tried to align your values, your words, and your actions with His. Just when you're in a good place, the stressors rear their ugly heads. This, my friend, is spiritual warfare.

Do you see a convergence of factors in the world today leading humanity down a narrow corridor of choice, being told there are only a few prescribed options "under the circumstances"? The truth is, there *are* forces converging, both in the world and in your personal life. The antichrist spirit that moves against the

> The antichrist spirit that moves against the Holy Spirit is already at work in the world and has been since the dawn of the Church Age.

Holy Spirit is already at work in the world and has been since the dawn of the Church Age. "This is the spirit of the Antichrist, which you heard was coming and now is in the world already" (1 John 4:3b). As Satan's time draws to a close, he is heating up his efforts of fear and deception to increase your stress and decrease your discernment.[123]

In light of our struggles, we need to be aware of the forces working against our eternal salvation and how they might show up, almost innocuously, in our everyday lives. As the Scripture highlights, the enemy is spiritual, but no less real. He may be "unseen" but he is no less effective. He synchronizes the efforts of the evil rulers and authorities of the unseen world, the mighty powers in the dark world, and the evil spirits in the heavenly places. Simply stated, we are engaged in battle, but not against flesh and blood. The Antichrist spirit is maneuvering us to make choices that fall in line with his deviant plan whether we realize it or not. Whether or not Satan is orchestrating our choices, he's definitely manipulating them for his advantage.

The enemy has a secret weapon and he is using it— oppression: the feeling we have of the walls caving in on us. It is palpable: isolation, loss, fear, and disillusionment. What can we do about it? Circumstances may not change in our lives or in the world, but the oppression we feel as a result *can* change. We can fight back against Satan's tyranny. We can find that centered place of peace that transcends our circumstances.

---

123 "Therefore, rejoice, O heavens and you who dwell in them! But woe to you, O earth and sea, for the devil has come down to you in great wrath, because he knows that his time is short!" (Revelation 12:12).

How do we find that place of unwavering? Answer: by creating a battle plan. I have sketched one for you below. These are the things you need to add to your life right now.

◈ FIND TRUTH

Truth forms the basis of our battle plan because everything, including our eternities, will be measured against it. By truth I don't mean *your* truth. I mean *the* truth. You might not even realize there is such a standard.

People adopt relative truths when we acquiesce to versions that rationalize sin. We have all done it. We tell ourselves that we are good people, at least better than most. You, for one, would never slight the feelings of another, at least not purposefully. You shudder at the thought of shunning what someone else values, as long as it feels good to them.

By truth I don't mean *your* truth. I mean *the* truth.

How can these seemingly "nice" and "tolerant" positions be wrong? The answer may surprise you: they show indifference to Jesus's sacrifice. Make no mistake; Satan will take advantage of our indifference.[124] Jesus says if you're not with Him, you're against Him (Matt. 12:30). There's no middle ground. The world naturally flows away from God. You have to purposefully take a stand to swim upstream against the world to follow Jesus. Jesus spits lukewarm Christians out of his mouth (Rev. 3:16).

---

124 "Be sober-minded; be watchful. Your adversary the devil prowls around like a roaring lion, seeking someone to devour" (1 Peter 5:8).

When we watch, even sigh, shrug our shoulders, or roll our eyes at relative truth, we are not defending God's Word.

When we don't stand for God's truth, we are actually aiding and abetting the enemy; we are coming up against Jesus. Aiding and abetting Satan doesn't happen in obvious ways. He knows it's too conspicuous to go around tempting people with horns and a pitchfork. He's insidious, creeping into our culture slowly, but deliberately.

Satan has deceived society into believing that what is right is wrong and what is wrong is right. He knows if he puts in the hard work up front, we will do the majority of the rest of the work for him. We will seek to validate and rationalize our sin, dragging others into the fray. Eventually, society will insulate

Satan has deceived society into believing that what is right is wrong and what is wrong is right.

Satan's egregious, despicable lies from the light of truth. And what we once knew was wrong, the majority will now claim is right.

Bottom line: Jesus is truth. "I am the way, the truth, and the life" (John 14:6). He deposits the Spirit of truth in believers. "When the Spirit of truth comes, he will guide you into all the truth, for he will not speak on his own authority, but whatever he hears he will speak, and he will declare to you the things that are to come" (John 16:13). Without truth, we can't know Jesus; without Jesus we can't know truth. How does Satan compare to truth? "When he lies, he speaks out of his own character, for he is a liar and the father of lies" (John 8:44b.). Satan is the anti-truth. As such, he is Antichrist. *Step 1: Find truth and stand by it.*

To fully know truth, take this time to accept Jesus as your Lord and Savior. Pray this prayer:

> *Dear Jesus, I believe you are the ultimate and only source of truth. I accept you as my Lord and Savior. I believe that you are God's Son and He raised you from the dead. Thank you for your sacrifice. Help me see truth and stand by it by living in faith no matter what life brings. In your great name, Amen.*

◈ GET GROUNDED IN THE WISDOM OF GOD'S WORD

The place to learn about God's truth is in the Bible. "Blessed is the one who finds wisdom, and the one who gets understanding, for the gain from her is better than gain from silver and her profit better than gold" (Prov. 3:13-14). What is your understanding of God and His plan of redemption? Did you even know He had a plan? Did you even know you needed redemption? Open the Bible and let the words transform you in ways you didn't think possible. "The Word of God is living and active, sharper than any two-edged sword, piercing to the division of soul and spirit, of joints and of marrow, and discerning the thoughts and intentions of the heart" (Heb. 4:12).

You might have been taught that the Bible is irrelevant to modern living. You may think the Bible is full of errors, being merely a human document. With sixty-six different authors, you believe it's merely a conglomerate of mortal ideas and thought, nothing more. In other words, the Bible, in your estimation, is untrustworthy and fallible.

The truth is, the Bible hasn't changed. It is the same today as it was thousands of years ago. The miracle of sixty-six books of the Bible by roughly forty different authors from different cultures, languages, and eras is that they do not contradict one another, as impossible as that sounds. To the extent they record the same events differently, that actually adds to the Bible's credibility. No two eyewitnesses describe one event exactly the same. To do so would raise suspicions that they were told what to say. The Bible is consistent and reliable.

Reading the Bible takes commitment, but it's not onerous. You will be filled with peace. If you can, commit to reading one chapter of one book each day, or even each week. Find a local Bible study and ask the tough questions. Really delve into the Bible's rich wisdom. You won't be disappointed. Don't have a Bible? There are organizations such as FreeBibles.net or BiblesforAmerica.org that will send you a free Bible. You should also be able to find one at your local church or library. Bottom line: "All Scripture is breathed out by

> Reading the Bible takes commitment, but it's not onerous. You will be filled with peace.

God and profitable for teaching, for reproof, for correction, and for training in righteousness" (2 Tim. 3:16). If you want discernment in a world of shifting sound bites, read your Bible. *Step 2: Find a Bible and read it.*

◈ TAKE EVERY THOUGHT CAPTIVE

God is not only concerned with how we act, but why we act. Thoughts are first conceived in the mind and then absorbed by the heart where they flow into our actions. If our heart gives birth to our words and actions, and our thoughts influence our heart, what gives birth to our thoughts?

You've heard it said that the mind is a battlefield. In order to guard our heart, we have to filter what we let into our minds. There are many doors to our mind: eye doors, ear doors, touch doors, taste doors, and smell doors.

How do we know what to filter out? We filter out any influence that wouldn't be present in heaven. With the bombardment of influences and temptations disguised as fun, the effort to guard our heart is easier said than done. Anything that stirs wrong desires in us must be avoided. This includes books, pictures, magazines, places, activities, people, talk, computers, drugs, food, etc.

God has our best interests in mind. He knows that as desirable as these doors seem to be, they will lead our life down the wrong course, ultimately to eternal death. Take the first step and *close that door.*

Take the first step and *close that door.*

Sometimes the enemy will plant negative thoughts. We don't have to take ownership of these, but once we do, they contaminate our heart, which gives birth to sinful words and actions. There is a step we can take when unwanted thoughts enter our mind. Paul teaches us to "take every thought captive to obey Christ" (2 Cor. 10:5). Only Jesus has the power to nail such sin to the cross. We cannot "handle" it on our own. That's why Paul didn't stop at "take every thought captive." Rebuke thoughts, words, and pronouncements made over you that do not conform with God's Word. Make them obey the ultimate authority—Jesus Christ. Bottom line: we have to know truth found in the Bible to give us the discernment to take captive those thoughts that aren't true. This is how we guard our hearts and stay faithful in a faithless world. *Step 3: Take every thought captive to the obedience of Jesus Christ.*

◇ PRAY IN JESUS'S NAME

This one may seem pretty innocuous, but it's very powerful. In fact, it's so significant, God taught me this in a vision when I was a little girl. The memory is clear to this day: A woman I loved like my mom sat me down and taught me, very specifically, to pray in Jesus's name. So from a very young age, I ended every prayer, "In Jesus's name, Amen." Since I was not familiar with the angelic world at that time, I attributed this lesson to my mother. One day, when I was a little older, I thanked my mom for such an invaluable lesson. She looked at me, confused, and said, "Sara, I have never heard such a thing myself. I did not know the Bible teaches us to pray in Jesus's name. How could I teach that to you?" My mother grew up in a Catholic school where such lessons were not part of the school curriculum or catechism. God knew I would need to harness that power to fight spiritual battles in my life. And you know what, it has always worked.

Jesus taught, "Whatever you ask in my name, this I will do, that the Father may be glorified in the Son" (John 14:13). God wants us to ask. He wants us to ask in His name because He is the one through whom it is possible for us to receive anything from God. It doesn't mean He only hears prayers in His name; I believe it means there is more power praying in His name. What's more, there is power over the principalities of this world and the evil spiritual realm when we speak Jesus's name. If you can pronounce "Jesus," you can make the demons flee from you. If that's all you can muster, muster His holy name.

Every morning lay hands on your children and ask God to guard them from harm that is seen and harm that is unseen. Pray for Jesus to fight their spiritual battles. Pray it all in Jesus's name. Every mealtime pray with thanksgiving for your daily portion of food and ask God to bless it. Every night lift up your requests to God with gratitude for the blessings of that day. Pray for the world, pray for His presence, pray for His values to pierce the spiritual veil, and pray for the salvation of others. Bottom line: Pray for everything, but add to the force behind the prayer by praying in the name of Jesus. Make the unclean spirits flee by proclaiming, "Jesus is my Lord and Savior." *Step 4: Pray in Jesus's name.*

◈ PRAYING AND FASTING

When I was in my late twenties a health crisis nearly killed me. After I had my first child, I began getting headaches behind my eyes. The sensation was one of a balloon being blown up, as if at any moment it would burst. Then one day, it did. My whole head felt like it exploded. My entire life shifted trajectory as a result. I had to quit my job as a lawyer. To be honest, there were times I thought death might be better than one more day with the unbearable pain.

Doctors did scans but couldn't find anything. I was left to figure it out on my own. The whole situation was embarrassing because I didn't have a medical explanation for what happened. Why would I suddenly quit my career? Why do I lay in bed all day?

I was desperate. Even though I was not totally familiar with Scripture, I had some knowledge of the power of fasting. After eight months of agony, I decided to take a day to fast and pray. It was less than a week later that a doctor actually called me with an idea. He prescribed shots of a medicine that immediately reduced severity of my headache.

The injections were a little out of the ordinary, but somehow, even though no other doctor had ever seen anything on my scans and even though every other doctor had lost interest in my case, this one particular doctor not only saw something, but decided to do something about it. In an interesting twist, he never saw anything on a scan again.

When the disciples could not exorcise a particular demon

from a possessed man, they asked Jesus why. Jesus responded that the disciples did not have enough faith. And then He added, "However, this kind does not go out except by prayer and fasting" (Matt. 17:21, NKJV). There is power in fasting and praying. When we empty ourselves of our flesh's needs and seek more of God's Spirit, the response is a spiritual power to move out stubborn strongholds in our life.

Fasting can take many different forms. I recently did a Daniel Fast. This is a diet that restricts food and drink choices to what Daniel ate when he refused to eat the Babylonian food in exile. You can pray and fast for hours, a day, a week, or however long is safe for you (after consulting a doctor). What you choose to fast from can vary as well. Water should never be restricted, but some people choose to do what is the hardest for them to forego. Whichever method you choose for fasting, don't forget the prayer. Bottom line: add fasting to your prayer in times of stress, doubt, difficulty, sickness, persecution, and to release strongholds. *Step 5: Pray and fast.*

◈ PUT ON THE ARMOR OF GOD

God knows we are in a spiritual battle. He would love to fight it for us, if we will acknowledge and turn it over to Him. When we do, He gives us specific action steps, both offensively and defensively. Our job is to fight the battles daily in His grace and strength, remembering that He has already won the war. Ephesians 6:13–24 outlines His strategy:

"Therefore take up the whole armor of God, that you may be able to withstand in the evil day, and having done all, to stand firm. Stand therefore, having fastened on the belt of truth, and having put on the breastplate of righteousness, and, as shoes for your feet, having put on the readiness given by the gospel of peace. In all circumstances take up the shield of faith, with which you can extinguish all the flaming darts of the evil one; and take the helmet of salvation, and the sword of the Spirit, which is the word of God, praying at all times in the Spirit, with all prayer and supplication."

We start with the belt of truth, which we addressed at the outset. Truth holds everything together just like a belt in the soldier's armor. Next, we put on the breastplate of righteousness. Breastplates protect the heart, which is the source of our words and actions. We talked about guarding our heart by closing the doors to the influences that do not please God. Then we take every thought captive and make it obedient to the standards of Jesus. As we go forth into the world, we take steps of peace but not indifference. Our shoes leave the marks of the Spirit like footprints of peace in the lives of others. Remember, Satan takes advantage of indifference, and Christ says He can't work with it. The devil is firing flaming darts at you. Put up your shield of faith to extinguish them. Faith undergirds our reality with the hope of what is to come—the promises of God that secure our blessed future with Him in heaven. Finally, we put on the helmet of salvation and the sword of the Spirit, which is the Word, the Bible. We filter out the bad influences and inundate our mind with the good—God's wisdom. God's wisdom lets us discern, dividing truth from fiction. Bottom line: the armor of God will enable us to stand against the schemes of the devil. Wear it daily. *Step 6: Put on the full armor of God.*

◈ WALK IN THE FRUIT OF THE SPIRIT

The fruit of the Spirit cannot be generated on our own. Such fruit is from the Holy Spirit. Included in these virtues are love, joy, peace, patience, kindness, goodness, faithfulness, gentleness and self-control (Gal. 5:22–23).

The interesting thing about the fruit of the Spirit is the order in which they are written. For God, everything flows from His holiness, the greatest manifestation of which is love. From His love we experience joy; His joy gives us peace; His peace generates patience; His patience engenders kindness; when He is kind, we know goodness; His goodness evidences His faithfulness; from His faithfulness flows gentleness, which inspires self-control in us.

Which of these do we have the most trouble with? Well, all of them, if we are honest. While they flow from the essence of God, they do not flow from the essence of humans. We have to conform to the image of Jesus Christ through the practice of self-control. As we exercise self-control, we are better able to move up the list, more or less, until we can love like God loves (even our enemies).

Fruit of the Spirit is a blessing for believers and gives unbelievers evidence that the Holy Spirit is present in the world through the exercise of these fruits in their lives, despite our circumstances. Develop self-control in order to develop the other fruit of the Spirit. God will enable you to do this as His Spirit fills you from the top down with His love. *Step 7: Walk in the fruit of the Spirit.*

◈ WORSHIP GOD

There may not be a more powerful offensive and defensive strategy against the forces of the dark spiritual realm than worship. Worship can happen in several ways. We will address two: obedience (actions) and words (praise). We worship our Heavenly Father for His holy grace, justice, hope. We praise His mercy and love that never runs out. We praise His sovereignty and might. The demons will flee as we audibly praise His holy name.

When we obey God, we worship Him. "Worship the LORD in the splendor of holiness; tremble before him, all the earth!" (Ps. 96:9). We show God that He is first in our life and we have committed to His ways. Sadly, believers and nonbelievers alike will use Scripture to distort God's truth and defend lies to validate their sinful desires. The nuances can be minute, but they are always significant. People will rationalize the guilt of having not done what they should have done or for having done what they knew they shouldn't. Accept the Bible for what it is and for what it says. Live consistently with God's Word and find that you will be blessed for it.

The most common perception of worship involves singing

His praises. Most churches have "worship" leaders in this sense. Examples of people worshipping with music and song are found throughout the Bible. "Sing praises to the LORD, for he has done gloriously; let this be made known in all the earth" (Isa. 12:5).

We want to worship God with both our audible praise as well as by our obedience. Praise God in the good times and in the bad. In particularly difficult seasons, put on praise music in your house, in your car, on your walk, and sing right along out loud. You are producing a force that cannot be tolerated by Satan. The demons will flee, leaving you with peace and a clear path to move forward in the direction of God's promises. Bottom line: Praise pushes back on the invisible forces of evil. Praise with obedience and with song. *Step 8: Praise God.*

CHAPTER

NINETEEN

NO FEAR

"For God gave us a spirit not of fear but
of power and love and self-control"

1 Timothy 1:7

I n the middle of 2020, I had a very vivid dream where I attended a special conference. I recognized three people from my neighborhood as I meandered the hallways before my session started. When it was about time to begin, I entered the conference room through the back doors. The room was large and dark with chairs set up in rows. The spotlight from above was directed at the stage. I found my seat just a few rows back from the podium.

The keynote speaker I believed to be Jesus Himself. He told us that the times we are entering will be more deep than wide. I asked myself, I wonder what He means? Jesus answered me as if I had spoken my question out loud. He replied, "It means the times will be swift, but terrible."

Friend, I don't know if this was directed at my life, or at

world events, or neither. Whatever it means, it sounds worth avoiding if possible. The saving grace of the message: the terrible won't last—it will be swift. Does terrible always equate with fear? Not with God. Whether the end of our time or the end of all time, we must remember not to fear. In fact, fear does not come from God. When we fear what's to come, we give a foothold to the devil. And if we give him an inch, he will take a yard.

We need not own the fear promulgated by the world. The future events God has planned are not the enemy. Fear is the enemy. Fear does not enable us to think clearly, discern wisely, or act measuredly. Fear of our circumstances is the devil's tactic to make us submit to him rather than to God. Reverential fear of God, however, keeps us obedient and fearless in a world that Jesus has already overcome.

When fear rises in your heart, take the steps the Apostle Paul sets forth:

> "Do not be anxious about anything, but in everything by prayer and supplication with thanksgiving let your requests be made known to God. And the peace of God, which surpasses all understanding, will guard your hearts and your minds in Christ Jesus" (Phil. 4:6-7).

Cast off the fear by substituting your thoughts with 1) prayer, 2) supplication, and 3) thanksgiving. Peace will fill the void where fear once resided. This is a very practical step you can incorporate into your life right now to guard your heart and mind in Christ Jesus.

It is natural to fear, just not necessary. When Jesus approached His disciples by literally walking on water in the middle of rough waters, they were frightened. The sight of a man gliding on top of the rough waves was unsettling. Jesus knew their fears. "But He said to them, "It is I, do not be afraid"" (John 6:20). Jesus didn't stop there. As soon as Jesus got in the boat, they found themselves at their destination. Jesus supernaturally got them where they needed to be to quiet their fears.

Jesus can calm your fears as well. The one you have been waiting for has arrived. He wants to get you where you need to be. If you haven't already, put your faith in Jesus and allow Him to quiet your fears of the present as well as the future.

Heavenly Father, I am ready. I believe Jesus is your Son whom you raised from the dead. I accept Him as the Lord and Savior of my life. I believe He is the promised Seed. He is the visible manifestation of You. I am ready to take up my cross daily and follow Him. I know life won't be easy, but I am willing to stay faithful to Jesus despite the risks. Please forgive me for all the ways I have done wrong. I humbly repent and receive your forgiveness. At the same time, I forgive those who have wronged me. Lord, thank you for your grace. Thank you for your justice. Thank you for giving me hope that through Jesus, the best is yet to come. In your precious name I pray, Amen.

You might be asking, now what? If you have received Christ as your Lord and Savior and would like to mature in your faith follow these steps:

1. **Join a church.** Not just any church, one who professes Jesus as the only way to salvation, reconciliation with God, and an eternity in heaven.

2. **Join a Bible study.** Again, not just any Bible study, but one that is true to the original author's message (as opposed to a culturally-sensitive or watered-down message). Bible studies help us to seek His wisdom. Wisdom is vital to our spiritual well being.

3. **Read the Bible.** "So faith comes from hearing, and hearing through the word of Christ" (Rom. 10:17). When the Bible was written, the majority of society did not have access to written material. Lessons were passed down orally. That is, in part, why Scripture says "hearing" rather than "reading." But reading is hearing the Word of God in your mind, which will be absorbed by your heart, and then affect your words and actions. Read the word of God to have its truths permeate your life.

4. **Abide in Christ.** There's a difference between accepting Jesus and abiding in Christ. Culturally, "accepting" carries the connotation, "we're cool with each other." "Abiding," however, goes many steps further and means continually drawing from Him as the source of your life choices and attitudes.

5. **Obey.** The fruit of abiding in Christ is obedience. Culture will tell you if it feels good, it is good. Don't believe it. Many of you who are reading this are living with a particular sin. Now—not tomorrow, not next

week, not when the weather turns, not when the holidays are over—turn away from this sin. Drop it like a hot potato!

6. **Find a Christian mentor.** A godly mentor will hold you accountable to your decision to turn from sin and follow Jesus. If you don't have a godly mentor, there are online organizations like Jesuscares.com or Groundwire.net, which have mentors ready to chat with you online to help you through a particular situation spiritually intact.

7. **Pray.** You can never have too much prayer. God wants a personal relationship with you so foster one by talking to Him. It doesn't have to be fancy. He already knows you, so be yourself. Be real. Be faithful.

MESSAGE FROM THE AUTHOR

"I make known the end from the beginning, from
ancient times, what is still to come. I say, "My
purpose will stand, and I will do all that I please.""

Isaiah 46:10

*E*schatology, or the study of the last things, is one of
the most contentious topics in theology. Those who
study the "last things" focus on prophecies that foretell
of events to occur at and after the end of the Church Age,
which is the time that we are living in right now (the Church
Age). As Scripture moves from the winding up to the winding
down of the world as we know it, eschatology hones in on the
consummation of God's plan to extend grace to sinners and
provide a path of covenantal blessing to both Jew and Gentile.
This blessing culminates with this significant event in history—
the Second Coming of Jesus Christ.

"Apologetics" takes its meaning from the Greek word
apologia and is translated "defense" or "vindication." Thus,
a simple definition of apologetics would be the discipline of
defending and/or advocating for the Christian faith using

rational arguments. Apologetics engages the mind and ties reason to faith. It seeks to help people develop a firmer commitment to God by eliminating intellectual barriers to Christianity. Apologetics employs our critical thinking skills to evaluate and construct rational arguments to achieve this goal.

Because humanity's meaning, purpose, and even goal to which we are striving has already been set by Jesus Christ (and in fact, *is* Jesus Christ), we can defend our faith by claiming the infallibility of the ultimate Author of the eschatological prophesies. An infallible God would never promise something He didn't intend to keep. Although God's essence is different than our imperfect human nature, we can rationally accept, at least conceptually, that an *infallible* (a.k.a. holy) God would follow through on what He promised to do.

Apologetics, therefore, must not shy away from using biblical prophecy as a weapon in its arsenal to battle intellectual obstacles to faith. The holy character of God as well as already fulfilled prophecy gives us a rational basis for future fulfillment of biblical prophecy. Moreover, in these times of fear and uncertainty, making a logical connection between God's plan and His holy (perfectly loving and just) character can provide comfort and relief, as well as facilitate belief. If we focus on the character of the One behind the plan, we can take heart knowing no matter how His justice unfolds, we are safe in His will.

God's plan evidences His very wise and intelligent nature. As such, His plan is not only a revelation from God, it is a revelation *of* God. Only a good, just, and holy God would share what is to come. Only a good, just, and holy God has nothing to hide, no sneaky "gotcha" that would throw His children for a loop. Rather, it's all there, prophesied in Scripture, unfolded in time, and laid out for the rational mind to either accept or reject.

So far, the ratio of God's prophetic prediction to fulfillment is one to one. Why is that ratio so much higher than the ratio of human predictions? As we discuss herein, God's holiness requires that He stand by His word. Period. For this reason, Christians and non-Christians alike would be wise to pay attention to the remaining prophecies to be fulfilled. No doubt the rate of fulfillment will continue unabated.

The future matters. Our future inheritance with God is the prize for which we are running. Humanity's greatest longing is to be reunited with God. God begins with the end in mind; and He informs us too. Apologetically speaking, it doesn't get much better than a sure thing to excite the rational journey toward reaping the eternal benefits of God's eschatological truth. Such revealed truth is practically useful, but also theoretically true.

To that end, the Second Coming of Jesus Christ offers believers comfort, but unbelievers—fear. Both extremes can work for the same goal of moving humanity closer to truth as

> Apologetically speaking, it doesn't get much better than a sure thing to excite the rational journey toward reaping the eternal benefits of God's eschatological truth.

each side seeks out the Source of comfort or the resolution for their discomfort. Eschatology can be the nudge that motivates us to remove the thorn in our flesh, seek the forgiveness of others, repent of our sin, and recognize our need for a Savior.

That said, those who pursue the study of eschatology must do so responsibly. Apologetics greatly aids this endeavor through the use of our reason. Responsible use of reason does not distort Scripture. Students and scholars who set dates will be proven wrong, for no one knows the date or time, not even Christ himself. For eschatology to serve as a tool in the toolbox of apologetics, the credibility and integrity of the Bible must be upheld. We defend the truth of the Christian faith by setting forth objectively true propositions of eschatology. False predictions can cause nonbelievers to doubt the truth of God's Word. A responsible apologist or theologian will not intentionally misrepresent the difficult-to-understand passages of Scripture, those that speak of future events, and especially those that do so using apocalyptic imagery. Instead, we are required to diligently study His whole Word (including prophecy) to extract its correct meaning and application to our lives.

Nothing in this book should be construed as predicting *exactly how* the Last Days (that is, the *end* of the Church Age and beyond) will play out. The focus is to be on specific aspects of God's character to help us better understand and trust His promises about what is to come. Some of the Bible passages from Daniel and Revelation may come across as rushed for this reason. It is not the purpose of this book to extrapolate on their fulfillment. I include them to give context and perspective. The important point—the prophecies *will* be fulfilled one way or another. We must be prepared.

When I wrote the initial draft for this book, I set forth a novel apologetic that ties the evidence of creation to a single source, the material world to the immaterial, and the physical to the metaphysical. The goal was to provide a rational basis to believe in God and; therefore, His promises. I removed it from this manuscript because I did not want the immediate message of God's character to which we cling in times of trial and tribulation to get lost in translation. What remains herein is a message of hope in our holy God whom we can and must trust: the best is yet to come. Those lulled to spiritual sleep in the time between one's salvation and one's end (of your life or of the Church Age) must awaken from their faithless slumber before it is too late.

Do you have intellectual barriers that prevent you from accepting God's plan of grace, justice, and hope? I encourage you to renew your mind to see the issues clearly, that is, with the end in mind. You don't want to miss out on the best that is yet to come.

Review Questions

1. Do you have fear about the future? Why or why not? See Psalm 27, 112:7, 118; Matthew 6:25-34; Philippians 4:6-7; 2 Timothy 1:7.

2. How is fear of the Lord different than fear of circumstances? See Psalm 111:10, 118:6; Proverbs 19:23; Matthew 10:28; Isaiah 41:13.

3. What does the Bible say about listening to ungodly accounts of the future from fortune-tellers, those who claim to talk to the dead, or psychics? See Leviticus 19:31, 20:6; 1 John 4:1; Deuteronomy 18:10-12.

4. Are our lives by chance? Is there any meaning or purpose to them? See Jeremiah 29:11; Psalm 139:13; Proverbs 16:4; Isaiah 55:11, Romans 8:28; Ephesians 2:10.

5. How have the current events in the world affected your life? What is your response? See Proverbs 29:25-26 and Romans 12:19.

6. Do you believe the future has already been written? How does that correspond with our free will? Proverbs 16:9 and John 15:16.

7. God already knows every free will decision we are going to make, so He directs them to fulfill His preordained purpose. Why does being within the will of God matter? See John 6:44, 7:17-18, 8:31-32.

◈ CHAPTER ONE

1. Did you, a family member, or a friend, experience any negative effects from the changes of 2020? If yes, how so?
2. Can you imagine circumstances in the world getting worse? Why or why not?
3. According to the reading what is the "Church Age"?
4. When someone says "End Times" what comes to your mind? Does the thought of separation from God being worse than cannibalism get your attention?
5. Believers in the first-century understood that the entire Church Age comprised the end times. The "end" of the end times will be a seven-year period known as what?
6. What happens at the midpoint of this seven-year period at the end of the Church Age? See Daniel 9:27 and Matthew 24:15.
7. What does Revelation say about whether people repent after the Seal judgments? See Revelation 6. The Trumpet judgments? See Revelation 9:20. The Bowl judgments? See Revelation 16:10-21.
8. Who are the elect? See Ephesians 1:4-5; Romans 8;29; John 15:16.
9. Does it provide you hope that God had the "elect" in mind when He cut the Tribulation Period short? Why or why not?
10. Do you believe that this life if not all there is? Do you trust God's version of the future?
11. What gives you peace during tribulation?

◈ **CHAPTER TWO**

1. What is the problem that needed to be solved?
2. Is anything unseen to God? What about to humans? How does the difference affect your faith? Proverbs 15:3; 1 John 3:20; Hebrews 11:1.
3. What was God's command about the Tree of Good and Evil? See Genesis 2:16-17.
4. How did Eve repeat God's command to the serpent? See Genesis 3:3. What does this reveal about Eve?
5. How did the serpent use Eve's twisting of God's words for his advantage? See Genesis 3:4.
6. How did Adam and Eve's knowledge of good and evil change their circumstances?
7. Spiritual death is the consequence of sin. Adam and Eve's sin opened the door for spiritual death for every person born after them. What is spiritual death?
8. What is the problem with entitlement? Do you see any consequences from the Age of Entitlement in our culture today?
9. Do you question God's commands? Do you see them as restricting your freedom or "fun"? How does an attitude of entitlement or pride fan the flame of such perception?
10. How could adopting a humble attitude change the quality of your reality today?

◈ CHAPTER THREE

1. How does God's story end? See Genesis 3:15.
2. Does the fact that God told us in advance help or hurt your faith?
3. What is the epic battle that all humans have to fight? Why doesn't God just eliminate the problem so we don't have to battle this anymore? See 2 Peter 3:9.
4. Do you fear death? How can shifting your focus from you life under the sun to your life yet to come alleviate your fear (considering God already told us how it will turn out)?
5. Look up the meaning of the name *Immanuel*. What does it stand for? How does the fact that the Messiah was prophesied to be Immanuel help your understanding of who He is?
6. How is the triune God (three persons in one) different than gods of pluralistic religions such as Greek mythology? See Deuteronomy 6:4 and 1 Corinthians 8:4-6.
7. How does Jesus's dual nature as both human and God enable Him to atone for our sins? See 1 Peter 3:18.
8. How did the prophesies of Isaiah 53 come true in history? How does it fulfill the promise in Genesis 3 about the Seed and the serpent?
9. How did the Promise of the Seed tie all of history together into God's redemptive story?
10. What is our role on earth until Jesus returns? 2 Corinthians 5:11, 20.

◆ CHAPTER FOUR

1. Do you believe God adjusts to our "new normals"? Why or why not? See Hebrews 13:8; Malachi 3:6; Isaiah 46:10.
2. How did contentment aid Franny Crosby in her blindness?
3. What is the biggest trial you have experienced or maybe are still experiencing? How can Franny's testimony give you hope to endure? Could you put your trial toward the good purpose of furthering God's kingdom?
4. Do you praise your Savior all the way through your trial?
5. Does it bother you that faith is the assurance of what we hope for and the conviction of things unseen? What about God's plan was visible and accounted for in history?
6. What does Jesus say about those who were not present to see with their naked eyes? See John 20:29.
7. In whom do those who do not have faith in God place their hope? How might this fall short?
8. Why is Jesus the only way to be saved from spiritual death? Why can't good people go to heaven? See Romans 3:23.
9. What if someone has not heard the Good News about Jesus Christ? Discuss Romans 1:19-20 and 2:14-15.
10. What is Satan's role in unbelief? 2 Corinthians 4:4.
11. What is our blessed assurance?

⬦ CHAPTER FIVE

1. What does God say about worry? See Matthew 6:27. What is the alternative He offers? See Matthew 11:28-30.

2. What is the list of seven things not present in heaven? Why is that a good thing?

3. When you read about spiritual death, what stood out the most to you? Why? How is it different than physical death?

4. How do we receive eternal life? See John 3:16; Romans 10:9, 13; John 3:36.

5. Can we accept Jesus and go about our lives the same as before? See John 14:12.

6. Write 1 Peter 5:10 in your own words.

7. Is pain real? Does God heal everyone who prays for healing? Why or why not?

8. What's the problem with temptation? Does God tempt us? See James 1:13-15. How do we resist temptation? 1 Corinthians 10:13.

9. Why is it important to tend to the physical needs of people to effectively witness about Jesus? What is more important: physical or spiritual hunger and thirst?

10. Why is human justice fickle? How do God's perfect notice, due process, and fair hearing change the justice outcome?

◈ **CHAPTER SIX**

1. How do we store up our treasure in heaven? 1 Corinthians 3:11-15.

2. What is the difference between the apocalyptic imagery of Revelation and other symbolism?

3. What did the angels tell the disciples after they watched Jesus ascend into heaven? See Acts 1:9-11.

4. If we want to thoroughly understand Revelation, where should we look and what should we study?

5. Should we believe those who predict the timing of Christ's return? Why or why not? See Matthew 24:44.

6. How does "Babylon" distract us from preparing for Christ's imminent return?

7. What will happen when Babylon falls?

8. What is of eternal value compared to the values of Babylon?

9. What in your life do you exalt above God? How can you change your priorities?

1. Do you harbor shame or guilt? How has Christ's sacrifice set you free? Can you claim this promise today? Why or why not?

2. Are you forgivable? How does Romans 8:1 clarify the source of our condemnation?

3. What is your perspective? Are you focused on all you have done wrong or focused on God's redemption? Colossians 3:2.

4. Fill in the blanks: Satan will _____ you for the very sin he _____ you into.

5. How does the story about Lot's wife in Genesis 19 warn us about looking at our past instead of on our future in Christ? See also Luke 9:62.

6. What stood out to you the most about Saul's conversion to Paul? See Acts 9.

7. What is God in the business of?

8. How do we position ourselves to receive God's forgiveness?
   a.
   b.
   c.

9. Read Psalm 51. Summarize the first six verses in your own words.

10. What does Colossians 3:13 have to do with God's forgiveness?

11. How does shame keep us from receiving God's gift of forgiveness? How has God shifted the focus from us to Jesus?

1. What can we anticipate in tribulation? See Matthew 5:10; 2 Corinthians 12:10; Philippians 4:6-7; 1 Peter 5:10.

2. Who experienced tribulation first? How has His tribulation enabled us to endure our tribulation? See John 15:18; 1 Peter 2:21; John 15:20.

3. What can believers anticipate at the end of the Church Age?

4. What does God's use of "marriage" symbolize?

5. How has culture defiled this most sacred institution of marriage to undermine this symbolism?

6. How do believers get to the Marriage Supper of the Lamb? 1 Thessalonians 4:16-18.

7. God is not clear about the timing of the Rapture. What should believers do if we have to suffer for our faith? James 1:12.

8. Do people get a second chance once the doors to the Marriage Supper have been closed?

9. If the Rapture occurs before the end of the Tribulation Period, can people still come to faith? How so?

◇ CHAPTER NINE

1. Is the end of the Church Age the very end of history? Why or why not? See Revelation 20:2-3.

2. What is the purpose of the Millennium? See Genesis 12:1-3 and Romans 9:4-5.

3. How long would the chosen people (Abraham's descendants) possess the land? See Genesis 13:15.

4. Is the Abrahamic covenant conditional? See Genesis 15 for the irrevocable ceremony with regard to this covenant and Ezekiel 20:40-44.

5. Is the land promised literal or figurative? See Genesis 15:18-21 and Deuteronomy 30:1-10.

6. One day the nation of Israel will possess the entire territory promised to them. One day, the Messiah will return to set up His throne, and through His righteous rule the whole world will be blessed with an abundance of peace, pleasure, and prosperity. How does the Millennium fulfill the promises of the Abrahamic covenant? See Revelation 20. See also, Ezekiel 36:22-37; Isaiah 11.

7. For believers present during the Millennium, what did they *not* do during their lifetime?

8. Where is Satan during the Millennium? Where is the False Prophet and the Antichrist? See Revelation 20:2-3.

9. What events precede Satan being finally relegated to utter darkness forever? See Revelation 20:7-10.

10. What era follows the Millennium? See Revelation 21.

11. Are believers and unbelievers alike judged by their works? See 2 Corinthians 5:10; Revelation 20:12. How do believers make it past the judgment with their works? 1 Corinthians 3:12-15; Rev. 19:8.

12. Are you prepared to suffer for your faith in Christ if necessary?

◇ CHAPTER TEN

1. What is holiness? See Psalm 96.
2. Who is holy? See Luke 1:49.
3. What does the holiness mean for God's promises? See Hebrews 6:13.
4. We are also called to be holy. Do we ever achieve God's level of holiness? What does the reading say about "empty promisors"?
5. How has your understanding of God changed in light of His holiness? Romans 8:32; Isaiah 46:10.
6. Where has God told us in Scripture that the best is yet to come? See examples from 1 Corinthians 2:9; Revelation 21:4, 22:1-5.
7. What three characteristics of God does this book focus on to understand the biblical events foretold at the end of the Church Age?
   a.
   b.
   c.
8. According to this chapter, what is the definition of "grace"?
9. What is the definition of "justice"?
10. The definition of "hope"?
11. How are we secured of Christ's victory now, even though we don't receive full possession until later?
12. How does God's patience mean your salvation?
13. Does God's holy grace and justice give you hope? Why or why not?

◇ **CHAPTER ELEVEN**

1. Do we have to go a certain amount of time without sinning before God will offer us salvation? See Romans 5:8.
2. What is the nicest thing someone has done for you? Did you deserve it?
3. How does the line between love and hate become blurred? How is God different?
4. How is grace different than mercy?
5. Who is the pre-eminent manifestation of God's grace? Why?
6. Do you require collateral to trust that someone will follow through with his or her promise? What would it take for you to accept God's plan of redemption through Jesus Christ?
7. In what ways has God's grace been sufficient for you?
8. Are you more like the Pharisees who think they "see" clearly by themselves or like the blind man who needed Jesus to be able to see the truth?
9. Do you believe in science? How is cultural science both compatible and incompatible with God and the Bible?
10. Have you ever mourned the end of a particular trial because you might not rely on God as much when times are easier?

◈ CHAPTER TWELVE

1. What are the wages of sin? In other words, what does sin "earn" us? See Romans 6:23.
2. How is justice represented by two sides of the same coin?
3. How do we reject God's love?
4. Are there any well-intentioned people?
5. What do you think of Spurgeon's quote: "Brother, if any man thinks ill of you, do not be angry with him; for you are worse than he think you to be."[125]
6. How does our free will play into which side of the coin you will be served?
7. Fill in the blanks: Redemptive: _____do, _____pay; Retributive:_____ do, _____pay.
8. How does subjective truth defined by culture lure us down the path to retributive justice?
9. Who serves our death sentence under redemptive justice? Retributive justice?
10. Which side of the justice coin will God serve you? Why?

---

125 Charles H. Spurgeon, *The Complete Works of Charles H. Spurgeon: Sermons 2001 to 2061*, vol. 34 (Fort Collins, CO: Delmarva Publications, 2013).

◆ CHAPTER THIRTEEN

1. Summarize 2 Thessalonians 1:6-7 in your own words.
2. How is it "just" to always get what we deserve?
3. Describe the "game changer" for believers getting what they deserve. See Proverbs 21:15; Romans 3:25-26.
4. Is it beneficial to fear the judgment at the end of the Church Age? Or the God behind the judgment? Why or why not?
5. What happened to King Belshazzar of Babylon? Why? See Daniel 5.
6. What happened to the Ninevites? Why? See Jonah 3.
7. How does Jesus balance the scales of justice?
8. Do you believe that God wants you to be saved? Do you believe you have had the opportunity to be saved? Do you believe you will have another chance to be saved after you die?

◇ CHAPTER FOURTEEN

1. What's the significance of a "living hope"? See 1 Peter 1:3.
2. What's the world's definition of "hope"?
3. Have you ever experienced a time of dashed expectations or lost hope?
4. Living hope is certain and secured, but still requires us to wait. Should we be discouraged? Why or why not?
5. How certain is Christ's resurrection? 1 Corinthians 15:20.
6. Is it good that physical death does not have the final say? How would your answer be different if you did not believe in Jesus?
7. Who is the authority behind the Bible's promises? How does holiness elevate that authority to an infallible standard?
8. What keeps us enduring in times of trial?
9. We want something that this world does not satisfy. What does C.S. Lewis say that signifies?

◈ CHAPTER FIFTEEN

1. Does Jesus provide signs that precede His Second Coming? See Matthew 24.

2. What are the extreme positions of those who study eschatology (end time prophesies)?

3. What is the "right" attitude to take regarding the timing of Jesus's return?

4. Review Matthew 24. Summarize the signs Jesus gave.

5. What danger have false predictions about the timing of Christ's return caused? How has scoffing also damaged people's awareness of Christ's return?

6. Summarize the signs given by Paul in 2 Timothy 3:1-7.

7. What happened in the days of Noah? What does that tell us about the attitude of those who will or will not recognize the signs at the end of the Church Age?

8. What are some possible interpretations of Daniel 12:4?

9. Read Matthew 24:32-35. If the fig tree is Israel, what significant event took place in 1948?

10. What stood out to you the most in the Parable of the Ten Virgins?

11. What stood out to you the most in the Parable of the Wheat and the Weeds?

12. What is the most important way we need to prepare for Christ's return?

◈ CHAPTER SIXTEEN

1. What is "love" according to 1 John 4:10?
2. Do you believe that God cares about you and what's going on in your life?
3. Can you relate to the lost sheep from Luke 15:3-7? How or how not?
4. Is it hard for you to choose between trusting God and trusting science? Is God sovereign over science?
5. What does the Bible say about creation? Is it described as a succession of flukes and random molecules haphazardly coming together to create life? See Genesis 1.
6. Can science answer for our morals and conscience? Why or why not?
7. What yoke does Christ offer? How does that differ from the yoke of this life? See Matthew 11:28-30.
8. Where are we instructed to place our spiritual eyes? Colossians 3:1.
9. Why do we fight God's rules when He knows what we need (after all, He created us)?
10. What can you do to pay your faith forward?

◈ CHAPTER SEVENTEEN

1. What kind of reward awaits us in heaven? See Matthew 5:12.
2. What chasm does Luke 16:26 describe?
3. What is heaven like?
4. Does it surprise you that "love" is the overwhelming memory of those who have experienced a NDE?
5. Does it surprise you that heaven is a literal place? Why or why not?
6. Imagine heaven with no sun or moon yet flooded with light. What kind of emotion does that bring forth in your heart?
7. Are you ready to be rid of evil? Are you afraid it might get boring without evil? Why is this not possible?
8. What can you imagine we will be able to do with our glorified bodies?
9. Does it matter to you that all things will be made new in heaven? Why or why not?

◈ Chapter Eighteen

1. Are you in need of a battle plan right now? What steps are you going to take?

2. How palpable is oppression in your life? Do you feel better knowing that circumstances may be out of your control, but oppression is within your control to change?

3. Do you believe truth is relative? Can you have your own truth? How is calling right wrong and wrong right a sign of the end times? See Isaiah 5:20-21; 2 Timothy 4:3.

4. Is the Bible relevant today? Why or why not? 2 Timothy 3:16-17.

5. What practical step can you take to renew your mind and take captive every thought to the obedience of Jesus Christ?

6. Have you ever prayed and fasted? What effect did it have on your circumstances and your heart?

7. What is your opinion about the fact that we are not fighting flesh and blood? Ephesians 6:13.

8. How is walking in obedience an act of worship?

9. How can you worship God today?

CHAPTER NINETEEN

1. Write 2 Timothy 3:12 in your own words. How has what we have learned about our future inheritance put this Scripture verse in the right perspective? See 1 Peter 3:14.

2. In whom will you place your trust for the future? Does God's holiness give you assurance you can trust His plan? Why or why not?

3. Do you think it matters to be in the will of God? How will your answer determine how God's plan affects you?

4. It is natural to fear, but not necessary for those redeemed by Jesus Christ. How do you respond to your circumstances? Your future?

5. Is there anything giving you anxiety that God's assurance in Philippians 4:6-7 can alleviate?

6. What steps can you take today to deepen your relationship with Jesus to calm your fears so you can focus on the best that is yet to come?

About the Author

S ara B. Anderson is a wife, mother of five, lawyer, ministry leader, and Christian apologist. Sara is author of 20/20 Vision: How Exodus 20:20 Brings the Purpose of Our Trials into Focus and president and founder of Fruits of Faith Ministries, Inc. Sara's great delight is spreading the truth of God's Word in the world. She sees fulfilled prophecy and the infallible, holy character of God as another tool to remove intellectual obstacles to accepting God's gift of faith in Jesus Christ.

Made in the USA
Middletown, DE
12 December 2020